HISTORY OF THE WORLD

The New World

CHERRYTREE BOOKS

A Cherrytree Book

This edition adapted by
A S Publishing

First published by Editoriale Jaca Book s.p.a. Milan
© Editoriale Jaca 1991
First English edition published in United States
by Steck-Vaughn Company
English translation © Raintree Publishers Limited Partnership,
a Division of Steck-Vaughn Company.

This edition first published 1994
by Cherrytree Press Ltd
a subsidiary of
The Chivers Company Ltd
Windsor Bridge Road
Bath, Avon BA2 3AX

British Library Cataloguing in Publication Data
Dambrosio, Monica
    New World.—(History of the World Series)
    I. Title   II. Barbieri, Roberto
    III. Williams, Brian   IV. Berselli, Remo
    V. Series
    909

    ISBN 0-7451-5233-3

Printed in Hong Kong by Imago Publishing Ltd

CONTENTS

A native North American. Despite the continent's huge size, the North American Indian cultures formed three main groups: the Eastern Woodland Indians, the Hunters of the Plains, and the Fishers of the North.

A seafarer from Southwest Alaska. The Aleuts, who lived in this area, had broken away from the Eskimos earlier in their history and had developed a culture that depended on the sea.

An Indian mask from the Northwest Coast (1500 B.C.). The coastal tribes were noted for their ability to carve and decorate wood.

GREENLAND

Beaufort Sea

Baffin Island

Alaska Range

Great Bear Lake

Great Slave Lake

Hudson Bay

Labrador

Newfoundland

Lake Winnipeg

Lake Superior

St. Lawrence River

Columbia River

Rocky Mountains

Lake Huron

Pacific Ocean

Missouri River

Central Lowlands

Lake Michigan

Ohio River

Appalachian Mountains

Atlantic Ocean

Sierra Nevada

Platte R.

Colorado R.

Arkansas R.

Canadian R.

Red R.

Colorado R.

Brazos R.

Mississippi R.

Florida

A Hopewell dignitary in ceremonial dress. The Hopewell civilization, (400 B.C.–A.D. 400) developed in the region that is now Ohio (USA).

Baja California

Eastern Sierra Madre

Western Sierra Madre

Rio Grande R.

Gulf of Mexico

Bahamas

Cuba

Hispaniola

Yucatan Peninsula

Caribbean Sea

Chimecoati, a god of the pre-Columbian period.

A Mayan sculpture of a priestess in front of a temple. The Mayan civilization, which began to develop around 500 B.C., produced very fine pottery. This civilization was already in decline at the beginning of the Spanish conquest.

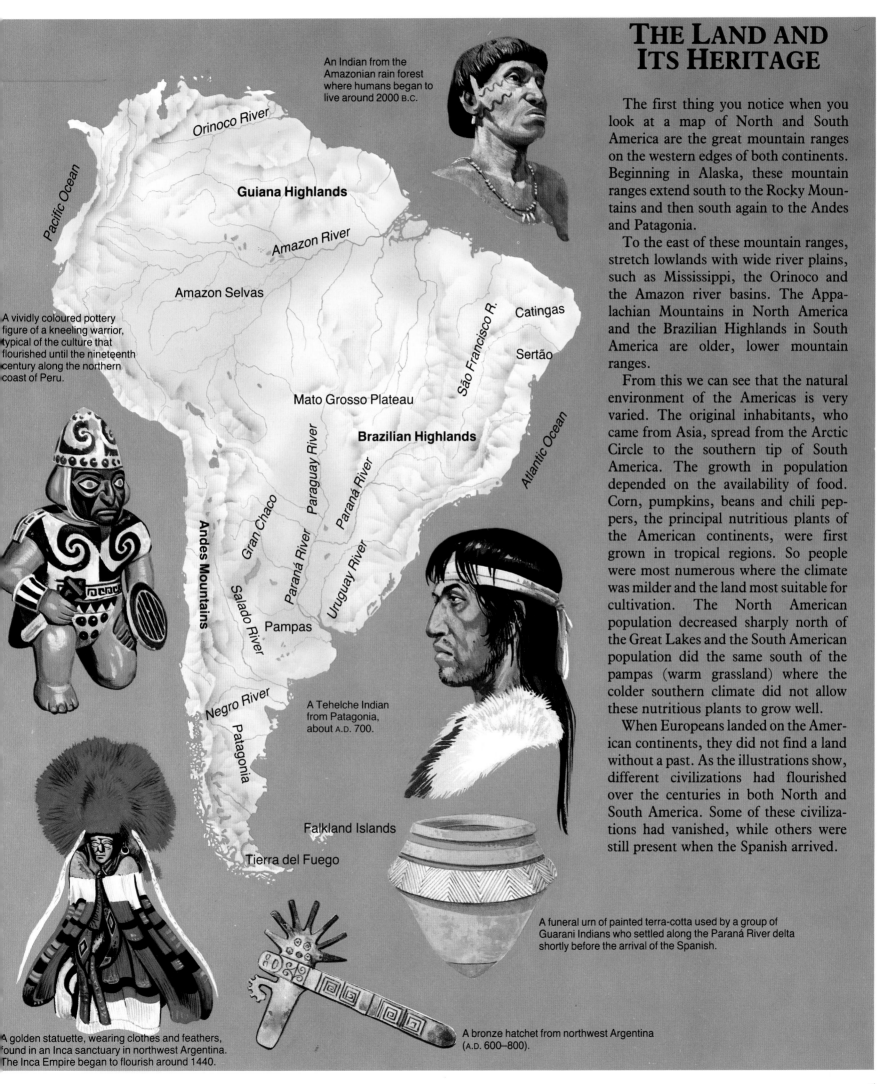

THE LAND AND ITS HERITAGE

An Indian from the Amazonian rain forest where humans began to live around 2000 B.C.

Orinoco River

Pacific Ocean

Guiana Highlands

Amazon River

Amazon Selvas

A vividly coloured pottery figure of a kneeling warrior, typical of the culture that flourished until the nineteenth century along the northern coast of Peru.

Catingas

São Francisco R.

Sertão

Mato Grosso Plateau

Brazilian Highlands

Atlantic Ocean

Andes Mountains

Gran Chaco

Paraguay River

Paraná River

Paraná River

Uruguay River

Salado River

Pampas

Negro River

Patagonia

A Tehelche Indian from Patagonia, about A.D. 700.

Falkland Islands

Tierra del Fuego

A golden statuette, wearing clothes and feathers, found in an Inca sanctuary in northwest Argentina. The Inca Empire began to flourish around 1440.

A bronze hatchet from northwest Argentina (A.D. 600–800).

A funeral urn of painted terra-cotta used by a group of Guarani Indians who settled along the Paraná River delta shortly before the arrival of the Spanish.

The first thing you notice when you look at a map of North and South America are the great mountain ranges on the western edges of both continents. Beginning in Alaska, these mountain ranges extend south to the Rocky Mountains and then south again to the Andes and Patagonia.

To the east of these mountain ranges, stretch lowlands with wide river plains, such as Mississippi, the Orinoco and the Amazon river basins. The Appalachian Mountains in North America and the Brazilian Highlands in South America are older, lower mountain ranges.

From this we can see that the natural environment of the Americas is very varied. The original inhabitants, who came from Asia, spread from the Arctic Circle to the southern tip of South America. The growth in population depended on the availability of food. Corn, pumpkins, beans and chili peppers, the principal nutritious plants of the American continents, were first grown in tropical regions. So people were most numerous where the climate was milder and the land most suitable for cultivation. The North American population decreased sharply north of the Great Lakes and the South American population did the same south of the pampas (warm grassland) where the colder southern climate did not allow these nutritious plants to grow well.

When Europeans landed on the American continents, they did not find a land without a past. As the illustrations show, different civilizations had flourished over the centuries in both North and South America. Some of these civilizations had vanished, while others were still present when the Spanish arrived.

PRE-COLUMBIAN CIVILIZATIONS

The First Americans

"Pre-Columbian" means "before Columbus". When Christopher Columbus arrived in the Americas in 1492, millions of people already lived there. Columbus called these people "Indians" because he thought he had landed in the Indies, islands off the southeastern coast of Asia. In Mexico, Central America and in the Andes Mountains, some of the most magnificent civilizations the world has ever known had developed and flourished, totally unknown by the people in Europe and Asia at the time. Many types of culture were present in the Americas: primitive societies of hunters and gatherers; simple societies based on agriculture; and powerful empires. Today a great part of this ancient splendour is lost because the European settlers and conquerors destroyed the native populations and evidence of their achievements. The early Americans had little chance against European technology, so much more advanced than their own.

At the time Columbus arrived, around four hundred languages were spoken in the Americas. With the exception of the Inuit, or Eskimo, language, no link between any ancient American language and the languages of Asia or Europe has been proven.

Scholars still disagree about how to estimate the total population and the exact number of languages spoken in the Americas, but most agree that people arrived on the American continent from Asia around thirty thousand years ago by crossing the Bering Strait. These first inhabitants of the American continent knew how to make tools and weapons and how to obtain food and shelter.

The Environment

The environment of the Americas is varied. There are huge mountains, broad plains and river basins on both continents. Before the arrival of Columbus, people were distributed widely over the habitable regions of both continents, from Greenland, where the Inuit lived, to the tip of South America.

The growth of population and civilizations in the Americas was dependent on the ability of food-plants to resist frost. The principal plants – corn, pumpkins, beans and chili – were of tropical origin, and the population became concentrated where cultivation of these plants was easiest, that is, in the temperate latitudes. For example, in eastern North America, corn was grown as far north as the Great Lakes, beyond which far fewer people lived. It was

Some of the most sophisticated civilizations of the New World flourished in Central America. *Centre page, left:* A religious statue made of jade and serpentine from the ancient Olmec civilization (1200–200 B.C.), and an Aztec warrior wearing the typical plumed headdress and black facial decorations.

The Inca Empire was the greatest in South America. *Lower left:* An aribal vase. This was a large vase, typical of the Incas, used for transporting liquids. (Painted clay, Pachacamac, A.D. 1400s.)

hardly by chance that the great pre-Columbian civilizations flourished in the warm zone between the Tropic of Cancer and the Tropic of Capricorn where the food was more plentiful.

Civilizations North and South

The most complex civilizations developed in Central America and in the Andes. Here rose highly-organized states, with monumental architecture and sculpture, together with state religions. In the southern part of Central America, and in Colombia, western Venezuela, and northern Ecuador, the civilizations were less sophisticated and were based primarily on agriculture. A similar pattern was evident in the Caribbean islands. Societies based on crop-growing also developed in the Mississippi River area, while tribal societies – whose economies were based on the cultivation of manioc – were present to the east of the Andes, and in the Orinoco and Amazon river basins.

A large number of tribes that existed by farming and hunting lived between the Atlantic coast of North America and the Great Lakes. The men hunted game, while the women tended the fields. Towards the west were the vast prairies, crossed by nomads in pursuit of bison, or buffalo. The horse-riding Plains Indian did not in fact appear until *after* Columbus. It seems most likely that at the end of the 1600s, the tribes living on the edge of the prairies found themselves displaced by the advance of the European colonies on the one hand and by more powerful Indian tribes on the other. This spread across the prairies would not have been possible without the horse which was reintroduced to North America by the Spanish. Wild horses had died out in the Americas long before.

The arid regions of the far west of what is now the United States were home to small groups of Indians who lived by gathering roots. Meanwhile on the Pacific coast a culture dependent on fishing for its survival had developed.

In the Americas, in general, there were many types of cultures, and the continent had such varied physical and climatic conditions that life for European settlers was a continuous adventure. For them it may truly be said that a "New World" had been discovered.

Above: The lid of an Aztec urn in gilded terracotta, on which traces of red and yellow paint are evident. *Right:* A Mayan monument in stone, about 4 metres high, situated in Copán, Honduras, and dating from the eighth century.

Left: The Inca city of Machu Picchu today: These ruins in Peru are an impressive monument to a vanished world.

An Inca warrior

The illustrations show some of the pre-Columbian people living throughout North and South America.

Top left: An Ipiutak hunter. The Ipiutaks settled in the Arctic. The igloo was the typical nomadic dwelling of these Arctic people, who lived by hunting and fishing. The smaller picture is of a harpoon tip made from walrus tusk.

Top right: A warrior beside a typical dwelling of the Eastern Woodland Indians, one of the most numerous groups of native Americans.

7

EUROPE DISCOVERS AMERICA

The First "Discoverers", The Vikings

The Vikings, who were expert seamen, lived in Europe between the ninth and eleventh centuries. From Scandinavia, the Vikings sailed across the North Sea into the Atlantic. Vikings settled in Iceland, which had been previously uninhabited, and ventured as far west as Greenland. From here, towards the end of the 900s, they reached Labrador and Newfoundland. The Vikings reached the coast of the North American continent, but the small colonies they founded died out.

Europe and the Wider World

Throughout the Middle Ages, Europe had kept its links with Asia. The Mongol Empire of the 1200s and 1300s had favoured contacts between Europe and the Far East. Trade was by land over the Silk Route, which merchants followed from Asia Minor to China.

This profitable trade was weakened with the rise of the Turkish Empire, which in the 1400s, extended from Asia Minor as far west as Egypt. This new, hostile Muslim power made it difficult for Europeans to reach India and China by the traditional overland trade routes. New routes had to be found. This search, aided greatly by new types of ships being built in Europe, triggered a series of geographical discoveries.

The New Vessels

The galley of the Mediterranean, an oared ship, was a useful cargo-carrier but unable to sail stormy seas. In Venice and Genoa another type of vessel was developed. It was bigger and higher, with two or three decks, three masts and a set of square and triangular sails. These ships could survive both storms and attacks by pirates because they were floating fortresses. Moreover, since the ships were so large, it was no longer necessary to put into port so frequently. Spain, Flanders or England could be reached directly from Genoa or Venice. In this way Italian, Spanish and Portuguese sailors, and later all western European sailors, learned the techniques of sailing on the high seas. The new ships combined the skills of European shipbuilders with techniques copied from the Arabs and other Eastern sailors. Called carracks and caravels, these excellent sailing ships could cross oceans.

Christopher Columbus

The reasons for the voyages to America in the 1400s may be found in the Europeans' desire to reach the riches of Asia, especially India and China, without having to cross Muslim territory. By this time many geographers knew that the earth was round and that it should be possible to reach Asia by sailing west across the Atlantic. Some scientific curiosity, but mostly a burning desire to reach the fabulous riches of the East, sharpened the Europeans' courage.

Christopher Columbus was born in Genoa (Italy) in 1451. He moved to Portugal in 1476, where he studied Portuguese navigation and shipbuilding methods. He visited Africa and England and in 1480 submitted to the Portuguese a plan to reach India or China by sailing westwards, across the Atlantic. At this time the Portuguese were more interested in exploring Africa, and they rejected Columbus' proposal. He presented his plan to the French and

The shortest route from Europe to the American continent, as shown on the map, was taken by the Vikings who reached the coasts of Labrador in the tenth century, but did not set up regular contacts with America.

Top of page: A Viking longship used for ocean crossings.

Main picture: In 1492 Columbus left Spain for Asia. He landed instead on an island in the Bahamas (the larger arrow on the map shows his route). His three ships were the *Santa Maria*, *Niña* and *Pinta*.

English kings, but with the same result. He then tried the Spanish court of Ferdinand and Isabella, and finally obtained their consent. Ferdinand and Isabella named Columbus governor of all the lands he might discover.

Columbus set sail from Spain in August 1492 with three ships. On October 12 he reached an island in the Bahamas that he named San Salvador. He began to explore the other islands in the archipelago, then sailing east, he visited Cuba and Hispaniola, where he left some members of his crew. On March 15, 1493, he returned to Spain where his voyage had begun. Columbus continued to believe he had reached eastern Asia. He did not realize that America was in fact a "New World".

THE EARLY VOYAGES OF EXPLORATION

Western Europe was amazed and almost incredulous at the news of the "discovery" of a New World and people accepted the idea slowly. For example, even twenty years after Columbus landed in America, mapmakers following Columbus' wishful thinking still insisted on denying the existence of the American continents and continued to draw maps on which the Americas were just part of Asia.

The vagueness and comparative lack of scientific precision of these times helps us understand both the shock felt by the western Europeans and the social climate at the time of the discovery. Columbus himself, who undertook another four voyages to the West Indies between 1492 and 1504, gave inexact or incorrect information about his findings. For example, he confused the plant agave for aloe, and turkeys for chickens. (Neither aloe nor chickens existed in America.) He shaped popular superstitions and confused notions, and recorded having seen mermaids and men with tails! During his third voyage, in 1498, on reaching the mouth of the Orinoco River, he was convinced he had arrived in the Garden of Eden, a paradise on earth.

On the basis of these vague, often incorrect, reports, a curious picture of the New World was drawn. There Europeans expected to find either hardship and death or an earthly paradise, filled with slaves, gold and adventure. The first conquerors set sail with these contrasting visions in mind.

The Americas Revealed

As soon as Columbus returned to Spain, Ferdinand and Isabella asked for his discoveries to be legally recognized. In 1493, the Spanish-born pope, Alexander VI, issued a papal bull, *Inter Caetera*. This document traced an imaginary line one hundred leagues (about 550 kilometres) west of the Azores and granted the Spanish sovereignty over all the lands that had been discovered, together with those that would be discovered beyond it. However, the Portuguese monarchy asked for the revision of the document granted to the Spanish. In 1494 the Treaty of Tordesillas was drawn up. A new boundary line separating the Spanish and Portuguese colonial empires was fixed, this time at a point roughly 2,000 kilometres west of the Cape Verde Islands.

Between 1502 and 1512, the Europeans (mostly Spanish) began their military exploration and domination of the Caribbean islands. Nicolas de Ovando seized Hispaniola (Santo

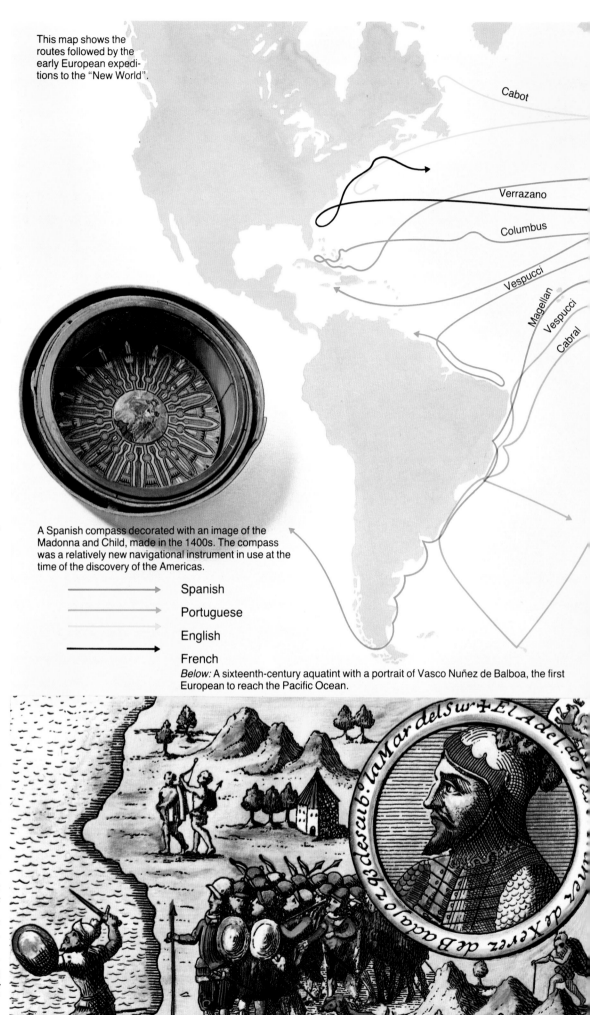

This map shows the routes followed by the early European expeditions to the "New World".

Cabot
Verrazano
Columbus
Vespucci
Magellan
Vespucci
Cabral

A Spanish compass decorated with an image of the Madonna and Child, made in the 1400s. The compass was a relatively new navigational instrument in use at the time of the discovery of the Americas.

⟶ Spanish
⟶ Portuguese
⟶ English
⟶ French

Below: A sixteenth-century aquatint with a portrait of Vasco Nuñez de Balboa, the first European to reach the Pacific Ocean.

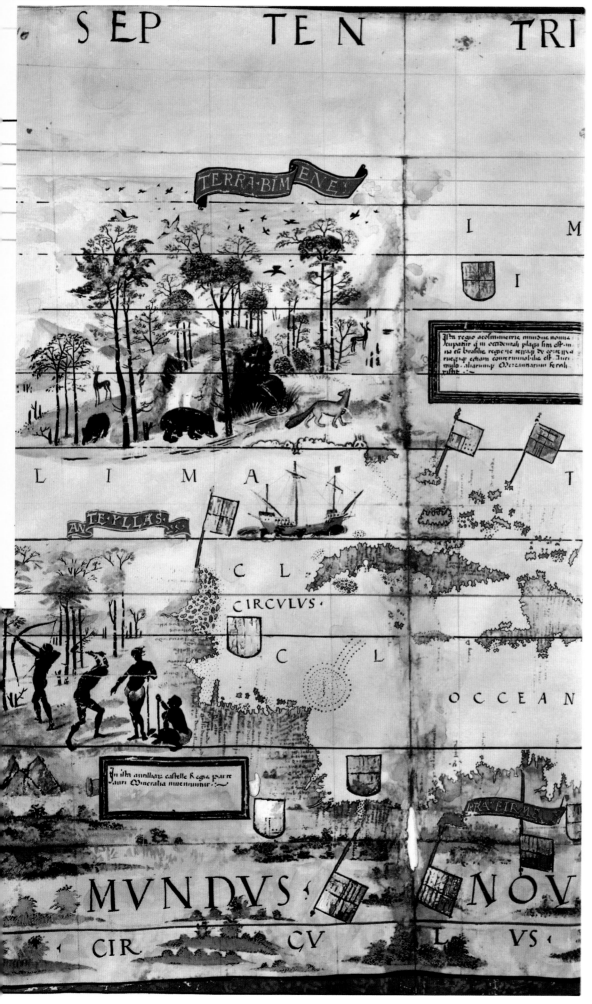

The New World as shown in an atlas printed in 1519.

Domingo) from 1502 to 1508. In 1509 Juan de Esquivel colonized Jamaica. Between 1511 and 1514 Diego de Velasquez and Juan Ponce de Leon conquered Cuba and Puerto Rico.

The leaders of the exploration of the Isthmus of Panama and part of the inland regions of what is now northern Colombia were members of the group that had accompanied Columbus on his first voyage. From 1497, Vicente Yáñez Pinzón explored the South American coast of the Caribbean Sea and then the coast of Brazil as far south as the Amazon River. The Isthmus of Panama and Colombia were reached by Rodrigo de Bastidas in 1500, Juan de la Cosa in 1504, and Alonso de Ojeda in 1508. In 1513, Vasco Nuñez de Balboa, after an exhausting twenty-day trek through swamps, forests, mountains, mud and torrential rain, became the first European to cross the Isthmus of Panama and reach the Pacific Ocean.

Between 1499 and 1502, the Florentine Amerigo Vespucci explored part of the South American coast. The reports of his voyage did much to enlighten the western Europeans about the new continent, which could no longer be confused with Asia. From about 1507, the continent became known as America, after "Amerigo".

In 1500 the Portuguese navigator Pedro Cabral landed in Brazil, while the Florentine Giovanni Caboto, better known as John Cabot, representing the English king, reached the North American continent in 1497. He was followed by Giovanni da Verrazano and Jacques Cartier, both in the service of the French king. In 1519 the expedition led by the Portuguese Ferdinand Magellan, sailing for Spain, completed the first circumnavigation of the globe. Magellan did not finish the trip, for he was killed in the Philippines.

In 1544 Francesco de Orellana explored the continent along the Marañón River – the Amazon. Between 1540 and 1554, Pedro de Valdivia explored Chile.

Europe's New Global Role

With the discovery and the conquest of the Americas, Europe (the smallest continent) began to establish contacts worldwide. The centre of economic gravity shifted gradually away from the European seas – the North, the Baltic and the Mediterranean – to the wider Atlantic and Pacific oceans.

World commerce increased enormously. Europe began to import new overseas products, such as potatoes, corn, tobacco and sugarcane. The exploration and exploitation of the New World boosted the rise of Spain and Portugal as nation-states, followed later by the Netherlands, France and England.

Cortés landed near what is now Veracruz, Mexico, in 1519. In general, the Spanish were welcomed by the local Indians who believed the white men were gods who came from the sea.

Central America at the time of the discoveries with the routes of Columbus and Cortés.

Cuba

Caribbean Sea

Aztec Empire

Mayas

Cortés 1519–1525
Columbus 1492–1493
Columbus 1502–1504

The conquistadors destroying the Aztec idols in the Temple of Cempoala, where human sacrifices were performed.

According to native legends, the coming of the Spanish was foretold by an omen, the passage of a comet.

A Mayan funeral urn used to hold human ashes, bearing an effigy of the goddess of water. (*Mayan Temple Museum, Mexico City*)

THE AGE OF THE CONQUISTADORS: MEXICO AND CENTRAL AMERICA

The Aztecs and Their Predecessors

At the beginning of the sixteenth century the Spanish invaded Mexico, and found there the Aztecs who ruled over a powerful empire. They had access to the Pacific and Atlantic oceans and controlled the main lines of communication in Central America. Backed by a powerful army, the Aztecs ruled their empire from their capital, Tenochtitlán, the site of modern Mexico City.

The empire was subdivided into administrative regions, each of which contributed taxes. The Aztec civilization developed an intensive system of agriculture, constructed many impressive buildings and temples, and formulated simple but exact theories of astronomy and a system of writing. Their writing was not based on sounds, but on pictures. Much importance was placed on religion, above all on the worship of the sun. Human sacrifice was a widespread practice.

Aztec society was rigid and static which, in part, explains the ease with which it was overthrown by the Spanish. The social structure included the Lord of Men (the king), the nobility, the powerful priest class, the merchants, the artisans, the peasant farmers and finally the slaves. Cortés conquered this powerful empire with the help of six hundred soldiers, sixteen horses, ten cannons, and thirteen arquebuses – an early form of musket.

The Spanish Conquerors

In Spanish history, 1492 was not only the year of the discovery of America. It was also the year that Granada, the last area of Muslim resistance in Spain, was conquered. This event marked the end of the *Reconquista* period of Spanish history, a period during which Christian forces in Spain brought to an end the Muslim domination of large areas.

The new monarchs ruling Spain were Ferdinand of Aragón and Isabella of Castile. They had managed to unite rival factions under a united crown. They put an end to the struggles between the nobles, who were granted important privileges for supporting the government of the kingdom.

The men who took part in the conquest of America came from all levels of society, but they all had one common wish – to find overseas the fortunes they lacked at home. Among these men were poorer nobles who had taken part in the Reconquista process, but who, at its end, had found themselves with few opportunities.

Several of these aristocrats had been ruined by the economic crisis that had hit Spain during the years immediately before the discovery of the Americas. It was not by chance that both Cortés and Pizarro came from Estremadura, one of the poorest regions of Spain.

For such men, America offered an opportunity to become rich and to perform heroic deeds. From often obscure backgrounds, they became "conquistadors" or conquerors.

Cortés' Conquest of Mexico

Hernán Cortés, born in 1485, landed in Santo Domingo in 1504. After a rather disappointing initial period on Santo Domingo, he became secretary to the governor of Cuba and in 1511 helped to check a revolt there. From this war he gained considerable experience in fighting the native people.

In 1519 Cortés left Cuba for Mexico. This marked the beginning of a new phase of the Spanish presence in Central America, which ended with the submission of the amazing empire dominated by Moctezuma, lord of the Aztecs. In April 1519, Cortés landed in Mexico and established the settlement of Veracruz as the base for his explorations. The local people welcomed him, believing that Cortés could help free them from the tyranny of the Aztecs. Cortés took advantage of the resentment these people felt for the Aztecs, who even demanded they supply human sacrifices for religious ceremonies. The Spaniard persuaded numbers of Mexicans to join his small army in overthrowing the Aztecs.

Cortés' next step was to use his superior weapons. The Aztecs were familiar neither with gunpowder nor horses. To understand Cortés' relatively rapid conquest of Mexico, it is important to appreciate the skill with which he used the weapons he had with him. He ordered his men to shoot their guns all together, to destroy trees and hillsides with cannon fire, and to make the greatest amount of noise possible. In this way he was able to terrify and confuse a much larger army. Cortés' venture ended bloodily in 1521 with the destruction of the Aztec capital and the massacre of its inhabitants.

For the next twenty years, the conquistadors continued their conquest of Central America. They also enslaved other peoples, including the Mayas, and explored farther south to the lesser known territories of Guatemala and Honduras.

THE AGE OF THE CONQUISTADORS: THE ANDES REGION

In the northern Andes, in present-day Colombia, lived the Chibcha people. They had ventured south as far as modern-day Ecuador, and north beyond the Isthmus of Panama as far as Nicaragua. The most developed regions were the Cauca River valley and the Bogotá Plateau, both in present-day Colombia. The Chibcha were ruled by despotic chiefs. In the Cauca River valley the people lived in small tribal groups, each headed by a lord. These were village-dwellers, with an economy based on agriculture.

To the south, the Inca Empire was the most powerful in ancient America. It was known as "the kingdom of the four points of the compass" – a kingdom that had no bounds. The Incas originated from the city of Cuzco, high on the Andean plateau. The spread of the Inca civilization began in the first half of the fifteenth century. Several nearby tribes asked for help from their powerful neighbour and soon found themselves absorbed into the kingdom of the Inca, the Lord of Cuzco. The Incas extended their rule over the entire region of the Andes, as far as central Ecuador. The Inca emperor, Tupac Yupanqui (1471–1493), conquered what we now call Bolivia and ventured into Chile and northwest Argentina.

Tupac's successor, Huayna Capac (1493–1527), pressed north, beyond present-day Quito. The empire extended as far north as the present-day southern frontier of Colombia and took in Ecuador, Peru and the Bolivian region of the Andes and Argentina, extending as far south as the Maule River in central Chile.

Pizarro Conquers Peru

Francisco Pizarro arrived in America from Spain in 1502. His military skills soon became apparent, and he took part in various expeditions. He was illiterate, which partly explains

why there are few written records of the conquest of Peru.

The contact between the Spanish and the Inca Empire was unlike the contact between the Spanish and the Central American civilizations. This time there was no surprise at finding a sophisticated civilization, only amazement at the sheer size and wealth of the empire.

Pizarro was obsessed with the idea of conquering Peru, but his first expedition (1524) was a total failure. Two years later he undertook a second voyage and in January 1527 reached Tumbes, a city overlooking the Gulf of Guayaquil, on the border between Peru and present-day Ecuador. The city was inhabited by an extremely civilized people, only too eager to exchange gifts with the small group of Spaniards. Pizarro received objects of gold and silver, textiles and ceramics.

He was informed that the Inca Huayna Capac had died in 1527, and that his two sons, Huascar, who lived in Cuzco, and Atahualpa, who lived in Quito, challenged each other for the throne. Pizarro decided to try another expedition and became involved in the Inca civil war (1531). In the battle of Cuzco, Atahualpa took his brother prisoner. The Spaniards first supported Atahualpa, but later took him prisoner and eventually killed him in 1533. After the death of the sovereign, the Inca Empire disintegrated.

By 1539, the Spanish controlled the empire, even though resistance continued until 1572, when the last Inca leader, Tupac Amaru, was killed by the Spanish. Peru attracted many opportunists, and its treasures held an irresistible fascination for the Spanish adventurers. They struggled among themselves to obtain the greatest quantity of the spoils of the conquest. These rivalries often led to civil wars, and Pizarro himself was killed on one such occasion. The reaction of the Spanish government was to send troops to deal with the rebels and put an end to these civil wars in 1542.

The horse was introduced to the American continents by the Spanish. Before the arrival of the Europeans, llamas were used to transport goods in Andean lands. The goods were left at a building that served as a relay station and warehouse. Beyond the building can be seen the circular terraced hillsides used by the Incas. This ingenious method of farming helped to develop a system of agriculture that could support a large population.

A hat typical of the Andes region.

An Inca knife. The handle represents a god of the heavens or of the moon. The figure was inlaid and painted, then beads and filigree were added. This object comes from the northern coast of Peru and is an example of the fine art produced by the Inca goldsmiths.

This Inca drawing shows peasant farmers using foot ploughs to prepare the land for sowing.

An Inca woman weaves cloth on a handloom. These looms were easily carried and could be hung up anywhere.

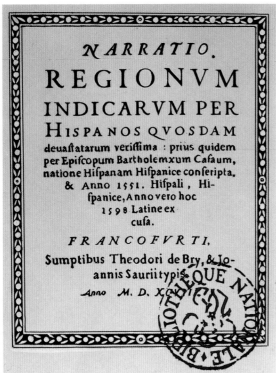

TREATMENT OF NATIVE AMERICANS

Cultures Destroyed

The arrival of the Spanish and their subsequent conquests were traumatic experiences for the native peoples of Central and South America. Their version of the conquest is recorded in fragments only. Some native Americans enlisted the help of the more sympathetic Spaniards, others learned to write in the Europeans' alphabet, and so preserved some account of the destruction of their people. Every report, chronicle, elegy or story is full of feelings of insecurity, misery and a progressively darkening sense of resignation.

By most estimates, the conquest reduced the native population of Central and South America in the sixteenth century by between 60 and 90 per cent. The conquistadors' behaviour towards the Indians was one of unprecedented cruelty. The Spanish destroyed villages and cities. They hanged, quartered, mutilated and burned alive men, women and children. The horror did not end there. Out of sheer desperation, to avoid falling live into Spanish hands, many natives actually hanged themselves or took poison, and there were many cases of mass suicide. If the tribes attempted to revolt, they were massacred.

Those who escaped murder were killed in other ways; by forced removal from their homes and hard labour, for which they were totally unprepared. They were defeated in military, social, cultural and psychological ways. They also suffered greatly from their lack of immunity to European diseases. Epidemics of smallpox were a scourge. Even measles, aggravated by exposure to the sun and by the habit of seeking relief by taking cold baths, claimed numerous victims. Many Indians died of influenza. The Spanish, in their turn, though in much smaller numbers, were plagued by rheumatic fevers and malaria.

A Sympathetic Voice

Bartolomé de Las Casas arrived in Santo Domingo in 1502. In the beginning, he lived like all the other Spaniards, enjoying the comfortable life that resulted from exploiting the natives. In 1511 he had a deep crisis of conscience and, the following year, he became a Roman Catholic priest. He then dedicated himself to defending the Indians' rights. In his book *A Short Account of the Destruction of the Indies*, published in 1552, he described the

The Conversion of the Indians

The sudden discovery in America of countless souls who had never heard of Jesus represented a challenge for the Roman Catholic church and for the Spanish crown. The work of conversion in the New World could only be entrusted to missionaries who were free from worldly ambitions. The church and the crown found the most suitable monks in the Franciscan, Dominican, and Augustinian orders, together with the Order of Mercy. These orders all had experience preaching to the poor and were highly disciplined organizations.

The first priests to reach the Americas had no precise programme for converting the Indians and had to overcome numerous obstacles. The native Americans did not understand Spanish, and none of the missionaries knew any of the local languages. The European priests were obliged to use hasty methods in the beginning. Later they set up communities in which the Indians were forced to live and receive instruction. Some missionaries learned Indian languages and studied their culture. Others despised both.

Converting the Indians proved difficult. The Indians were baptized and given religious instruction, but it is difficult to say how many were really Christian. Even those who witnessed the process had differing opinions on the subject. The Jesuits, for example, who arrived in America after the early missionaries, were convinced that the Indians were Christians only in appearance and professed the faith only for fear of punishment. It is likely that the Indians adopted Christian rites and teachings that were nearest to their spiritual needs and to their way of life. In this way, an American Christianity developed in which elements of old beliefs and customs survive.

horrors of the conquest and criticized Europeans who regarded the Indians as inferior beings. Just before his death in 1566, he wrote *The History of the Indies*, in which he recognized the value of the pre-Columbian civilizations. Sadly, despite his good intentions, by the time his writings became widely known, it was too late. The native Americans had already been subjugated or annihilated.

The Roman Catholic Church and the Americas

The discovery of America had a considerable effect on religious thinking in Europe. Christian Europe was surprised, confused and unprepared when faced with the existence of native Americans. The Bible clearly stated that the voice of God had arrived everywhere. Saint Paul's Epistle to the Romans stressed that there were no people who had not heard the Word of God. But then who were these "Indios", these peoples who were ignorant of the Word of God? What was to be done with them? They could be converted with patience, or by force, or they could be treated like animals lacking any form of rationality.

Those who supported the theory of conversion to Christianity without the use of force attempted to halt the violence of the soldiers. They appealed to the Spanish monarchs and to the pope for help. The spread of Protestantism in seventeenth-century Europe actually stimulated conversion of the Indians. Roman Catholicism, under pressure in Europe due to the Protestant Reformation, could now find new strength in America. But some priests and missionaries who accompanied the conquistadors took part directly in the destruction, plunder and exploitation of the Indians.

The Spanish took only a relatively short period of time to consolidate their empire due to the speed with which the settlers began to exploit the lands they had conquered. The Spanish Empire was a bureaucracy, in which full-time government officials administered a system ordered by the monarch. The chief seat of government in Spanish America was the viceroyalty. In 1535 the Viceroyalty of New Spain was created and took in all the territories north of Panama. In 1542 the Viceroyalty of Peru was created: it covered all the lands south of the Isthmus of Panama except for the coast of Venezuela.

The founding and development of towns was a typical feature of Spanish American colonization. Town life was based on the towns of Spain. It also allowed the crown more control over the colonies.

This scene shows the port of Havana in Cuba, one of the main centres of intercontinental trade. Colonial goods, such as tobacco, sugar, cotton, timber and silver, left this port for Spain. Goods from Spain would arrive here and then be distributed to other Spanish American colonies. In this region of the New World, native American slaves were soon replaced by slaves from Africa who were imported to do the hardest work.

THE FIRST SPANISH COLONIES IN THE AMERICAS

Spanish America

The exploration and conquest of Spanish America was accompanied by a slow but continuous build-up of a governmental bureaucracy. Spain claimed sole sovereignty over the new lands. In the beginning, however, it granted rights to the exploration, occupation and administration of territories to private individuals. The first obstacle to efficient control was the length of the voyage between Spain and the New World. Ships took about sixty days to reach the Caribbean islands from Cadiz, Spain, and from eighty to one hundred days for the return trip. It was therefore easy for the few thousand Spanish settlers in the new territories to avoid total obedience to any orders from Spain.

The Spanish government moved quickly to begin the development of the American lands. In 1503 the *Casa de Contratación* was founded in Seville. This organization was responsible for drawing up lists of passengers, goods and contracts for exploration. The Casa was charged with checking on and organizing emigration to the Americas. Anyone who wished to go had to have the approval of this organization.

Individuals and families emigrated to the Americas for different reasons: to make their fortune, to improve their social position, to escape justice, to serve God as missionaries, to serve the king as officers, or to accompany or find a husband. The crown, in fact, encouraged the emigration of women because it considered the Christian family the basis of the type of society it wished to create in the New World. Between 1540 and 1579, artisans, tradespeople, missionaries and government officials began to emigrate to the Americas. In 1511 the Council of the Indies was created to help the Spanish crown administer the new possessions. The treasurers, accountants and councillors set to work to oversee the activities of the conquistadors and to look after the interests of the crown.

The "Encomiendas"

The social structure in the Spanish possessions in the Americas was founded on the system of the *encomiendas*. This was an arrangement common in Spain, in towns, villages and monasteries under the dominion of the crown. The monarch assigned the administration of a certain amount of land to a deserving person for a fixed period of time. The assignee had the right to collect taxes for the crown from anyone living on the land and to request the inhabitants to carry out work necessary to ensure the *encomienda* was efficiently run. The concession was temporary and the land remained the property of the crown. Through the *encomienda*, the beneficiary collected for his own use a large proportion of the taxes the Indians were supposed to pay to the Spanish government. The taxes were both in the form of money and goods. Often the Indians were too poor to pay and were forced to work free for the *encomendero*, or tax-collector, who was supposed to give them protection and instruction in return.

In reality, this system in America degenerated into a system of slavery. Its abuses were condemned by the church and it was subject to ever-increasing controls from Spain. The condemnation of clergy like de Las Casas was accompanied by the concern of the crown, which was anxious to avoid the creation of a Spanish-American aristocracy. In 1512 the Laws of Burgos condemned the slavery of Indians, but the laws were never enforced.

Colonial Towns

A typical feature of Spanish colonization was the creation of towns. Fortified towns offered better defence and easier communication. The founding of towns and cities was part of the Spanish way of life and in the Americas town-building symbolized Spain's desire to keep the colonies under control.

In 1501, the king requested the governor of Hispaniola, Nicolas de Ovando, to create a city on the island. Ovando built San Domingo. The city had straight streets that crossed each other at right angles, modelled on Spanish cities built during the Middle Ages. The Spanish government rapidly issued general rules for the construction of urban centres in the Americas. The town plan should be like a chessboard: squares, streets and blocks of houses had to be built in straight lines. The starting point would be the central square, and the street system would develop from this point. This type of town planning became typical of the Spanish American cities. Despite this policy, however, many colonists spread into the countryside, and as the Spanish colonies developed, there were more Spanish-speakers living in the countryside than in the towns.

SEAFARERS, TRADERS AND PRIVATEERS

Throughout the entire sixteenth century, the French, Dutch and English explored North America and established settlements there. By the end of the century, these three nations had become powerful enough to challenge Spain. Their economies had growing needs for raw materials, and merchants gained an increasing amount of influence on governments. The settlements on the American continents provided furs, dyes, animal skins, plantation crops and sometimes precious metals.

During the seventeenth century, Holland became a shipbuilding centre. The Dutch vessels were fast, seaworthy and heavily armed

against pirates. The Dutch were such good constructors of warships that foreign powers made increasing use of their services. The naval powers of the northern European nations had grown to rival that of Spain and Portugal.

Despite the improvement in navigational techniques, life on board ship during the long ocean crossings remained very hard. The daily tasks the sailors had to perform were often dangerous, and sickness, in particular scurvy, claimed many victims among the crews. The living conditions often drove them to mutiny against their captains, a crime that carried the death penalty.

In the sixteenth century, adventurous captains from England, France and Holland began to penetrate American waters. Fast ships made frequent attacks on the Spanish domains in the Caribbean Sea and along the Brazilian coast. Ships regularly attacked convoys of Spanish merchant ships heading for Europe. Their favourite targets were the Spanish galleons carrying gold and other precious metals from American mines. The Spanish viewed these attacks as outright acts of piracy, which many of them were.

The quarrels in Europe between the Spanish king Philip II and the English queen Elizabeth I

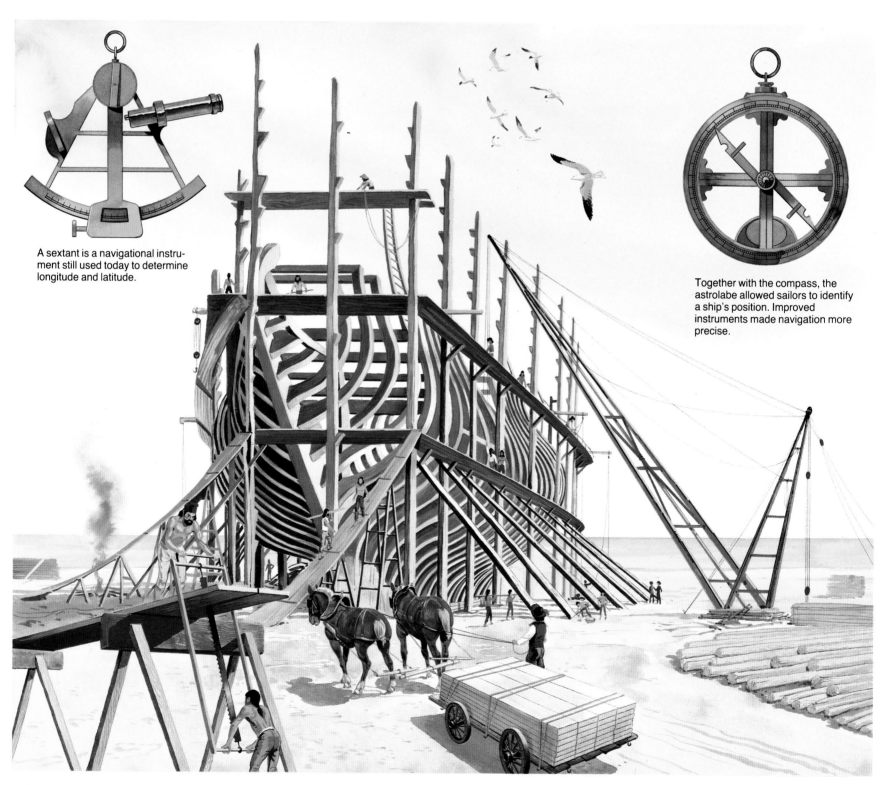

A sextant is a navigational instrument still used today to determine longitude and latitude.

Together with the compass, the astrolabe allowed sailors to identify a ship's position. Improved instruments made navigation more precise.

led to outbreaks of violence at sea, to the detriment of the Spanish trade with the colonies. This undeclared war brought considerable gains for the English crown. English raiding ships, or privateers, were not officially in the service of the queen. Their captains were adventurers who risked their ships (and lives) in pursuit of treasure. If their actions provoked embarrassment, the English government repudiated them. If the attacks on the Spanish galleons met with success, the booty was shared with the queen. The attacks in American waters were more the result of the enterprising spirit of audacious privateers, rather than the initiative of the crown. Thanks to them, England crippled Spain's merchant fleet in a relatively short time.

Government or Freedom?

The privateers did not always limit their efforts to attacks on ships. They raided land bases and roamed unknown stretches of ocean. Their captains were often able explorers. Sir Francis Drake circumnavigated the globe in three years (1577–1580).

From the beginning, the northern Europeans' approach to the colonization of the Americas differed radically from the Spanish occupation. The Spanish Empire was conquered through greed, the quest for adventure and the missionaries' desire to convert the Indians to Roman Catholicism. But it was also the result of a notable administrative effort.

The establishment of the power of the Spanish crown in the Americas began almost immediately after Columbus' first journey. Nothing similar was ever set up by the northern Europeans in their American dominions. The Dutch, for example, were primarily interested in founding trading posts. No central power interfered in the administration of these American possessions.

In the English settlements, the authority of the crown and of parliament was very superficial. The government rarely managed, or desired, to control the political life of the colonies. These initial differences had a lasting influence on the development of the colonies that eventually became the United States.

Opposite Page: A naval shipyard in Holland. In the seventeenth century, Holland became Europe's leading shipbuilder. Dutch merchant vessels were fast and well suited to the long ocean crossings. The Dutch also became the best builders of warships, and foreign powers made use of Dutch techniques and experience when building their own fleets of warships.

This Page: Ships of the Dutch West Indies Company. For the most part, the Dutch did not establish many permanent colonies in the Americas, but preferred setting up trading posts along the coasts.

THE PORTUGUESE IN AMERICA

Portuguese Expansion in Africa and Asia

Portuguese expansion, supported directly by the crown, began in 1415 with the conquest of Ceuta, Morocco. The Portuguese thus hoped to secure direct access to the riches of Africa south of the Sahara. Up to this time, the Arabs had acted as intermediaries for the trade in gold, spices, ivory and slaves. After the capture of Ceuta, the Portuguese began to explore the west coast of Africa, where they soon set up trading posts for the collection of gold, ivory and slaves. They established colonies based on the cultivation of sugarcane on the Atlantic islands of Madeira, the Azores and Cape Verde.

In 1498 the Portuguese expedition begun by Vasco da Gama reached India by sea. The Portuguese also took control of the Indian Ocean from the various Indian and Muslim rulers and kept control despite frequent attacks from the Turks. This supremacy was made possible by the construction of ports defended by stone fortresses. The most important of these bases was Goa in India. The majority of the local states were forced to pay taxes and sell their products to the Portuguese at fixed prices. The Portuguese eventually continued their Far Eastern explorations as far as Indonesia, China and Japan.

Map of Bahia, drawn around 1616. Bahia was the first capital of Brazil.

The port of Lisbon in the sixteenth century, based on an illustration of the time. Lisbon, together with Amsterdam in the Netherlands, was then one of Europe's main ports for trade with Africa and the Americas.

Portuguese Colonies in America

In 1500 the Portuguese explorer Pedro Cabral claimed the land now known as Brazil for Portugal. Compared to the riches discovered by the Spanish in Mexico and Peru, Brazil was a disappointment. It remained a third-rate colony for a long time, exploited primarily for its excellent timber. The first Portuguese settlements were little more than simple trading posts. Only in 1534 did the Portuguese king John III decide to colonize Brazil seriously. He divided his American dominions into "captaincies". Each consisted of a strip of coastline suitable for establishing a port plus an amount of territory stretching from the coast into the interior. These areas were assigned to people willing to commit themselves to colonize the territory at their own expense. In return, the settlers received economic and political rights within the area. The leader of the colony obtained the title of governor and captain and was allowed to govern his territory without interference from the king's officials. He also had the right to establish new towns and cities and to administer justice. In addition, there was a grant of economic privileges. He was exempt from paying taxes, and a fifth of the territory became his personal property. The remainder belonged to the crown, but the governor-captain could divide this land among his followers.

Two obstacles to this type of colonization were the hostility of the Indians, whom the Portuguese tried to reduce to slavery, and the ungovernable masses of Portuguese immigrants. Many of these arrivals were exiled criminals.

The Governor-General and Portuguese Emigration

The difficulties encountered in the attempts by the immigrants at colonization persuaded the king to reinforce his administration in Brazil. A royal settlement office was founded from which the governor was expected to co-ordinate the activity of the captaincies conceded to private individuals. The royal office was established in Bahia, which became the first capital of Brazil. After 1565, a second royal office was founded in Rio de Janeiro.

The government did not check or control immigration to the American colonies. There was an early policy of forced emigration for criminals and rebellious nobles. Colonial governors had difficulty in keeping these exiles under control. In Portugal, there was a shortage of labour, so few peasants emigrated. They had work enough at home. Instead, many migrants were impoverished aristocrats who emigrated to Brazil, together with their servants. They came with the intention of creating huge plantations for the cultivation of sugarcane or cotton. When the first governor-general was selected, a law was introduced prohibiting the creation of vast estates. However, the law was not enforced, and some estates reached colossal proportions, especially in the northern provinces.

Portuguese laws restricting immigration to their colonies were much less severe than the Spanish ones. Foreigners were granted freedom of trade and other privileges. Converted Jews were allowed to settle there. It was only at the time of the union between the Spanish and Portuguese crowns, 1580–1640, that Brazil was closed to foreigners.

Far left: A boundary stone marking the Brazilian possessions of the king of Portugal (sixteenth century). Compared with the riches found by the Spanish in Mexico and Peru, Brazil seemed disappointing. The first Portuguese settlements were therefore simple trading posts.

Left: Slaves working in a Brazilian sugar refinery. Despite the opposition of the crown, vast estates developed in Brazil, where sugarcane and cotton were grown. African slaves were shipped in to work on the estates, and Portuguese merchants were active in the slave trade.

Below: The Church of Saints Cosma and Damiano of Igaragu in Pernambuco was the first Brazilian church.

FRENCH SETTLEMENTS IN THE AMERICAS

The Antilles (West Indies)

In 1628 the French joined the English in settling the island of St. Christopher in the West Indies. Colonists cultivated tobacco and sugarcane, products which were much in demand in Europe. The French went on to colonize Martinique and Guadeloupe in 1635 and part of Santo Domingo in 1655.

The French islands became prosperous rapidly and were soon part of a system of international trade. The French bought slaves in Africa, sold them in the West Indies to work on the sugar and tobacco plantations, and exported the highly desirable colonial products to Europe. With the profits, the colonists were able to buy goods manufactured in Europe.

The relationship between the colonies and France was, however, not easy. Under Jean Baptiste Colbert, finance minister in the government of Louis XIV (1643–1715), there was a system of rigid state control of the economy, according to the principles of mercantilism. This doctrine declared that a nation should establish colonies to provide the raw materials it lacked and to serve as markets for the manufactured goods it produced. In this way, money would circulate between the nation and its colonies and would not enrich rival powers.

Colbert declared that colonial products should be exported only to France and that only goods made in France should be imported by the colonies. Thus, the colonies were no longer free to sell their products to the highest bidder or to buy goods at the cheapest price. To escape France's rigid economic policy, the French colonists resorted to smuggling and organized several revolts against France.

New France

The French had begun to explore North America around 1541, when Jacques Cartier landed in Canada. In 1608 Samuel de Champlain founded a successful colony in Quebec and created a settlement at Montreal. From here the French pushed south to reach the Great Lakes region and the Hudson River. From 1670 to 1685, due to the initiative of the fur traders, missionaries and adventurers, New France expanded to include the region along the Mississippi River south to its delta.

From the time of Louis XIV, France tried to gain more profits from its North American territories, which lay between those belonging to Spain and those belonging to England. But France's interest in them remained sporadic, and the French living in North America often felt abandoned by their government. The areas settled by the French proved poor in precious metals, and Canada in particular was too cold to produce the tropical products of sugar and tobacco so popular with the European market. Furs from the northern colonies were the main goods in demand in Europe.

America continued to be remote from French affairs, and only about sixty thousand French colonists emigrated to the New World, mostly labourers, orphans and soldiers.

French Louisiana

The entire Mississippi River basin was claimed for France in 1682 by the explorer Robert de La Salle and was named Louisiana in honour of the French king. The first permanent French settlement in the area was set up in 1699, when Pierre le Moyne founded the colony of Biloxi in what is now the state of Mississippi. At the beginning of the eighteenth century, the principal settlement moved to Mobile, in what is now Alabama.

For almost fifty years, the political life of Louisiana was dominated by Jean Baptiste le Moyne, who was nicknamed the "father of Louisiana". He was governor several times, and in 1718 he founded the city of New Orleans. The city became the capital of Louisiana in 1722. Relatively few Europeans settled in French North America. In 1750, when the English colonies boasted one and a half million inhabitants, the French population had reached only around eighty thousand.

The French in South America

As early as 1504, several French ships appeared off the Brazilian coast and attacked Portuguese trading posts. Between 1520 and 1530, the French became more aggressive and their raids caused considerable damage to the Portuguese settlements. However, although they founded the colony of French Guiana, the French never developed larger permanent settlements in South America.

Opposite Page, Left: The open-air trading post in Quebec, Canada. On market days native Americans came to exchange goods with the French. In return for beaver skins, the Indians received hats, glass beads and metal goods.

Left Top: Slaves being sold in a market in the French Antilles. The French made huge profits from the slave trade. Slaves captured by French merchants in Africa were sold to colonists in the Antilles. The African slaves laboured in the sugar and cotton plantations of the West Indies.

Left: A tobacco manufacturer in France. Tobacco, together with sugar and cotton, was one of the chief products imported to France from its American possessions.

DUTCH NAVAL AND COMMERCIAL POWER

The Development of a New Colonial Power

During the first half of the seventeenth century, the Dutch managed to create a vast trade network that extended throughout the world. Their large ships were able to transport all kinds of cargoes. Whatever and wherever goods had to be carried, from the more traditional products like pepper to the new products from both the North and South American colonies (sugar, tea, coffee and rum) the Dutch were present. Their fleet made up 80 per cent of all European merchant shipping.

In 1602 a number of Dutch trading companies merged to form a single company – the Dutch East India Company. This organization was entirely the result of the initiative of the Dutch middle class. It was an enterprise created by merchants, operating as a trading company able to make use of the energetic and practical qualities of its members. While the Dutch lived in sumptuous houses, they maintained a sober and thrifty life-style. They had a well-developed social system and supported schools, charitable institutions and orphanages.

The policy of commercial expansion went hand in hand with the undermining of Portuguese competition. Little by little, the Dutch managed to obtain a monopoly of trade in Southeast Asia. The Dutch toppled the Portuguese but imitated their style. Instead of penetrating territories and establishing real colonial settlements, as the Spanish did, the Dutch, for the most part, built trading posts on the coasts of Asia, Africa and the Americas. Exceptions to this policy were the colony founded in 1619 in Indonesia, around Batavia (present-day Djakarta), the permanent settlement of a group of colonists in 1652 near the Cape of Good Hope, and the founding of New Amsterdam (now New York City) in 1623. The trading activities of the Dutch merchants were accompanied by intense geographic exploration. For example, Dutch seamen explored the coast of Australia.

The vast commercial traffic run by the Dutch East India Company was controlled from Amsterdam, which became the point of exchange between distant markets. From Amsterdam, it was possible to see for the first time a truly world market emerging.

The Dutch in America

The first Dutch expeditions set out for the Americas in the sixteenth century. The Dutch were at war with Spain, and this enmity was also felt overseas. Between 1580 and 1640, privateers from the Dutch West Indies Company attacked the Spanish Silver Fleet. These ships transported the gold and silver mined in the Americas across the Atlantic to Spain.

The Portuguese colonial empire in South America suffered, too, from Dutch competition. By 1630 the Dutch had captured the city of Bahia and six captaincies in Brazil. These territories were important for the exploitation of Brazil's sugarcane and coffee, and for the slave trade. Recife became the chief Dutch base for the defence of the northeastern coasts of South America, but the city was recaptured by the Portuguese in 1654. The Dutch also conquered Curaçao in 1634 and Guiana (now Surinam) in 1636.

In 1609, the Englishman Henry Hudson, in the service of the Dutch, crossed the Atlantic Ocean. Like others before him, he hoped to find a northwest passage (for ships) through the North American continent that would lead to China. Hudson sailed up part of a river hoping it would be the northwest passage. It was not, but eventually the river would be named after him. Hudson's journey was of historic importance. In 1623 the Dutch decided to settle the area that he had explored. In particular, they settled the island of Manhattan, at the river's mouth. In 1626, Peter Minuit officially purchased Manhattan Island from the native Americans. New Amsterdam – present-day New York City – founded by a Dutch merchant company, became an important centre for the fur trade. The Hudson River was used as a route by native Americans of the northeastern forests who came with their furs to trade in the new settlement.

New Amsterdam flourished under Dutch control until 1664 when it was captured by the English and renamed New York.

Top: The port of Amsterdam. In 1579 the seven northern provinces, which became the Netherlands, declared their independence from Spain, which did not recognize the state until 1648. Amsterdam was a city of merchants and a lively cultural centre.

Far left: Gateway of Fort Orange, in Brazil. Here the Portuguese colonial empire suffered from competition with the Dutch. The Dutch captured the city of Bahia and six other settlements by 1630.

Left: New Amsterdam as shown in a sketch dating from the late 1600s. The city was founded by the Dutch in 1623. New Amsterdam was an important centre for the fur trade, and later became New York.

THE ENGLISH IN THE NEW WORLD

Elizabethan England

The reign of Queen Mary I, between 1553 and 1558, was a troubled time for England. Mary was a Catholic, and in 1534 she married King Philip II of Spain. She attempted to restore the power of the Roman Catholic church in England by persecuting English Protestants. This policy earned her the nickname "Bloody Mary". Her pro-Spanish politics led England to accept passively King Philip II's economic and political monopoly of the Atlantic Ocean. Her religious persecutions and her pro-Spanish attitude also made many English people identify Roman Catholicism with foreign interests.

Mary died in 1558. The new queen, Elizabeth I, who reigned between 1558 and 1603, was the daughter of Henry VIII and Anne Boleyn. She prudently achieved a change in the English approach to foreign policy and religion without resorting to fanaticism. An example of her diplomacy was the way in which she managed to modify her position regarding Philip II. The Spanish king proposed marriage to her precisely when she was beginning to change Mary's pro-Spanish, pro-Roman Catholic policy. Elizabeth refused Philip's offer, but also continued to refuse all other illustrious suitors, and, eventually, decided never to marry. Elizabeth re-established the authority of the crown over the church and restored the use of the Book of Common Prayer. In this way, she re-established Protestantism and the Anglican church.

In European affairs, Elizabeth eventually clearly arrayed herself on the side of the Protestant, anti-Spanish forces. England became the ally of the United Provinces in their struggle against Spain. The English rupture with Spain was inevitable. In 1588 Philip II prepared an invasion fleet of 130 ships, the Invincible Armada, which engaged the English fleet in the English Channel. The Spanish were driven back by English ships and many ships were destroyed by a storm.

England began to realize the political and military advantages of being an island. England stayed out of continental politics as much as possible and only occasionally helped the weaker contestant in European power struggles, to ensure the balance of power on the continent. The experience of the war with Spain served to strengthen the political and spiritual unity of England. It mobilized England's energy towards mercantile and seafaring activities and led to a period of colonial expansion.

The English in the Americas

The privateering exploits of great explorers like Francis Drake, John Hawkins and Martin Frobisher helped England penetrate the American continent. The efforts of Walter Raleigh led to the start of English settlements in North America in 1585, in the region the English named Virginia, in honour of Queen Elizabeth I. Raleigh's enterprise on Roanoke Island was a failure, but England had a group of leaders ready to continue the process of colonization. They were the younger sons of English landowners. They were educated and some were accustomed to the sea from their early childhood. In addition, there were large numbers of jobless or discontented English, willing to emigrate. Powerful merchants, willing to finance overseas ventures, joined forces with the landowning noblemen. The crown guaranteed the legal standing of the future colonies but did not wish to extend government control directly over the new lands. The settlements would be expected to govern themselves with little interference from England.

The English settlement of North America proved extremely difficult in the beginning because of the harsh living conditions. In 1607 a group of colonists landed in Virginia on a half submerged island surrounded by swamps about 50 kilometres up the James River. This unlikely place, named Jamestown (after King James I), was the first permanent English colony in North America. The population of the colony was soon reduced by the harsh environment, Indian attacks, sickness and general discouragement. Those who survived were bent on making a profit from the land and increasing their possessions. They desired to clear more forests, but there were not enough labourers to do the work. So the colonists devised a system of free passage from England to America for any farm workers willing to agree to work on the plantations for four years without pay. At the end of this contract period, the majority of these workers joined the ranks of independent tobacco growers and stayed in the colonies.

An English pirate ship attacking a Spanish galleon. The riches carried from the Spanish colonies lured pirates and privateers to attack the Spanish merchant ships.

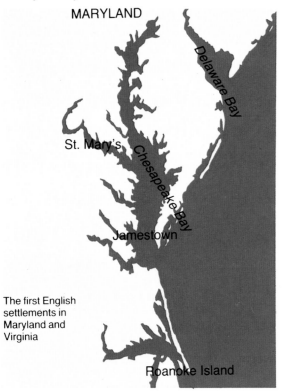

The first English settlements in Maryland and Virginia

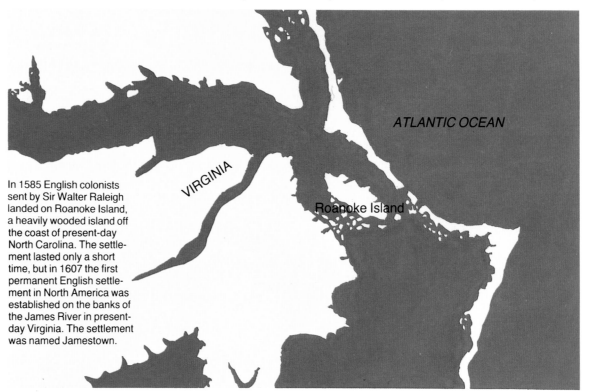

In 1585 English colonists sent by Sir Walter Raleigh landed on Roanoke Island, a heavily wooded island off the coast of present-day North Carolina. The settlement lasted only a short time, but in 1607 the first permanent English settlement in North America was established on the banks of the James River in present-day Virginia. The settlement was named Jamestown.

THE PILGRIMS AND THE PURITANS

The *Mayflower* and the Colony at Plymouth

In England, two "nonconformist" religious groups, the Pilgrims and the Puritans, sought to reform the Protestant Church of England, through a more direct approach to God. The Puritans were convinced that the English Church was still too "Catholic" and immoral. The Pilgrims developed as a separate sect in England between 1570 and 1580. They did not accept the authority of the Church of England and established their own churches. As a result, they were persecuted by both the official church and by the government.

In 1609 a group of Pilgrims decided to move to more tolerant Holland, where they were able to practise their beliefs freely. However, they began to worry that their children might be too influenced by Dutch society, which they judged as being too permissive. In 1619 the Pilgrims obtained permission from the Virginia Company to settle in its territory. They also received a guarantee from the English government that they would not be persecuted.

The Pilgrims sold their lands and property to finance their enterprise, and on September 16, 1620, they set sail from the English port of Plymouth on board a ship named the *Mayflower*. On November 21, the *Mayflower* dropped anchor in what is now Provincetown, Massachusetts. The passengers were so exhausted by the voyage that they decided not to proceed to the lands in Virginia which they had been promised. Instead, they sailed farther along the coast. On December 26, they went ashore and decided to establish a settlement. They called their colony Plymouth.

Other settlers followed in the wake of the *Mayflower*, and by 1657 there were over a thousand colonists in Plymouth. The political structure of the colony was extremely simple. The men met once a year to elect a governor and various officials. The governor of the colony

did not have authority from the crown to create a sufficient number of new towns and churches to receive all the new arrivals.

The Puritans in America

The Puritans in England were proud, enterprising and uncompromising with both themselves and others. Between 1628 and 1630 Puritan relationships with the English government and the Church of England completely deteriorated. In 1628 a group of Puritans formed the New England Company, which obtained a concession to a large part of the region that is now the states of Massachusetts and New Hampshire. In 1629 the Puritans were granted a charter by the English government to found the Massachusetts Bay Company.

In the summer of 1629, the worsening political situation in England, aggravated by an economic crisis, made the Puritans' position even more difficult. Charles I dissolved Parliament, thus making the possibility of political reform extremely remote. All Puritans holding administrative positions in the government were dismissed. A group of these, made up of merchants, landowners, lawyers and government officials, who were no longer able to share in the privileges of others, decided to flee to North America to live according to their Puritan principles. They hoped to create a new society, based on Christian values.

March 1630 marked the beginning of Puritan emigration. During the period of greatest exodus, 1630–1643, more than twenty thousand English Puritans reached North America. The original colony, Salem, on Cape Ann in what is now Massachusetts, became the clearing station for the new arrivals. They then settled chiefly around Charlestown and Boston. Later, some Puritans established independent settlements in Hartford, Wethersfield and Windsor, which joined together to form the colony of Connecticut.

Indian women harvesting maize, or sweetcorn. The English learned from the Indians how to grow corn and other plants unknown to Europeans.

The Pilgrims' first winter in North America after emigrating from England in 1620 was very difficult. They faced winter snows and hunger. Many of the original settlers died. The Pilgrims, like the Puritans who followed, had permission from the English crown to emigrate overseas where they hoped to practise their religion freely.

New plants such as tobacco, potatoes, peppers, maize (corn) and tomatoes, were introduced into the Old World from America. The importing of these products changed European diet and customs. Potatoes and corn, for example, became staple foods of many people in Europe. The habit of sniffing snuff spread rapidly, and tobacco was imported in ever-increasing quantities.

THE FAILURE OF THE DUTCH IN NORTH AMERICA

New Amsterdam

The population of New Amsterdam grew slowly and by 1664 had reached fifteen hundred. By the middle of the seventeenth century, the village included a blockhouse, a windmill and several houses. These were circled by a stockade, which served as a town wall, exactly where Wall Street in New York City is today. A canal ran around the edge of the settlement and about fifty small farms were scattered just outside the village.

The Dutch West Indies Company was convinced that it could continue to make a profit from the fur trade alone. The furs were easily transported down the Hudson, Delaware and Connecticut rivers. The company officials believed it would be useless and costly to attempt the creation of an agricultural community. They were sure of earning more money, and faster, just from the fur trade. So they made no serious effort to increase the population of the colony.

The War Against the Native Americans

However, back in the Netherlands, one of the company directors tried to assure a more secure future for the North American settlement. Kiliaen van Rensselaer, a rich Amsterdam jeweller, was convinced that large, private agricultural estates should be created there. These would guarantee food, livestock and supplies for the Dutch ships bound for the other Dutch possessions in the Americas. The result was the formation of twelve groups of financiers ready to back the creation of large farms. Only one venture was successful, the estate situated at Rensselaerswyck, on the banks of the Hudson River near Fort Orange (present-day Albany). The financier sent goods, livestock and farm equipment to the estate. In addition, he arranged for whole families of farm workers to emigrate, at his own expense. The estate developed and survived until the end of the century.

Unfortunately, as a whole, the colony of New Netherland, which consisted of parts of what are now Connecticut, New Jersey, New York and Delaware, was in difficulty. The governors

A meeting of Dutch merchants, whose main interest in North America lay in trade, not settlement.

compagnie Souveraine des Indes

sent by the Dutch West Indies Company were often inefficient and corrupt. One of them, named Willem Kieft, personally began a ruthless war against the local population.

The conflict began in 1642, after Indians attacked several isolated farms. In retaliation, more than a hundred peaceful American Indians camping near New Amsterdam were massacred. The war raged for three years until, in the end, the Dutch carried out a night attack on an Indian village, brutally killing and burning alive around five hundred inhabitants. A peace treaty was finally drawn up between the Dutch and the native Americans in 1646.

The Dutch and the English

The province of New Netherland remained badly organized, badly administered and disorderly. The lack of order was partly due to the uncontrolled multiplication of villages, which were too small to organize or defend themselves. These villages sprang up everywhere: in the upper region of Manhattan Island (New Harlem); along the banks of the Harlem River, in the area known today as Westchester County, New York; along the Hudson River, in the present-day region of Bergen County, New Jersey; and on Long Island.

The confusion was accentuated in these settlements because of conflicts with English neighbours who had moved to New Netherland from the neighbouring colonies. These immigrants were attracted by the promises of freedom to worship, self-government and free land. But the English began to rebel against Dutch domination and demanded English control over the frontier areas. The ensuing conflicts over the frontier territories became serious enough to force the colonies of New Netherland and New England to reach an official agreement in which the frontier with Connecticut was fixed at 16 kilometres east of the Hudson River.

But English colonists in Dutch-controlled areas ignored or opposed Dutch rule. Finally, in 1654, the Dutch West Indies Company went broke. All that remained of New Amsterdam were several moorings, a few bridges, a ruined fort and an abandoned town hall. The English colonists in Connecticut planned the occupation of New Netherland and invaded the frontier territories. In 1664 the Dutch colony had no resources left with which to meet the challenge of the English who had little difficulty in conquering New Amsterdam.

Squabbles and fights were commonplace in New Amsterdam. The Dutch had little control over the traders of various nationalities who settled there and in the other small settlements of Dutch North America.

Chinook

Klikitat

Yakima

Before the arrival of Europeans, the native Americans had developed four basic cultures. To the east of the Mississippi, as far as the Atlantic, lived tribes of hunters and farmers. The central prairies were the domain of nomadic hunters who followed herds of bison as they migrated. The pueblos, villages built by agricultural peoples, were found in the southwest. When the Europeans arrived, there were more than one hundred pueblos. In the northwest lived tribes that depended mostly on fishing and hunting.

Karok

Sioux

Cheyenne

Crow

Bannock

Sioux

Sioux

Sauk and Fox

Winnebago

Maidu

Pomo

Ute

Paiute

Pawnee

Osage

Navajo

Pueblo

Hopi

Iowa

Quapaw

Chumash

Apache

Cherokee

Comanche

THE ENGLISH COLONISTS AND THE NATIVE AMERICANS

Many cave drawings have been found in North America. Below are a few examples of the symbols found and their possible meanings.

Passamaquoddy

Iroquois

Wampanoag

Ottawa

Potawatomi

Iroquois

Pequot

Susquehanna

Delaware

Powhatan

Cherokee

Catawba

Creek

Choctaw

Seminole

◇ peace

●—● conversation / communication

▲ arrowhead

⌒ far from anywhere

rain

night

grandfather

the four compass points

war

snake/demon

shadows

circuit/turn

empty

piled

heart

to lift something

part

hill

light

a covered place

object

wooden object

strength

upward

Trading with the Native Americans

The colonists and the native Americans had difficulty in understanding each other. Their ways were very different. For example, the Europeans felt that the Indians were too affectionate with their children and never punished them for disobedience. The Indians, on the other hand, were horrified to see the colonists hitting their children with whips or belts. They were convinced the colonists behaved in this way to teach their offspring that the world belonged to the most violent. Their attitudes towards work were totally different. The fur merchants who worked for the large European companies lived among the tribes, spoke their languages, and did everything in their power to induce the Americans to dedicate themselves more seriously to hunting the animals whose pelts were in demand. But the Indians saw little point in killing more animals just for the sake of profit.

It was no easy task to persuade the Americans to hunt more, and so increase the production of furs. They were not greedy for money and had little interest in the cheap trade goods they were offered. In the end, the merchants found that introducing the Americans to whisky was the most effective stimulus. As time went by, contact with the Europeans made more Americans anxious to own European manufactured goods, and many left their camps to live near forts or alongside the trails where the merchants' wagons passed. The Americans received their first guns from English and French merchants. Possessing firearms gave the eastern tribes – the first of the North American Indians to have contact with Europeans – an advantage in their periodic wars with rival tribes from the interior of the continent.

Native American Clashes with the English Colonists

In 1607 when the Virginia Company, led by John Smith, founded Jamestown, the English colonists immediately clashed with Powhatan, a powerful Indian chief in the region. After only a few years, there were no native Americans left in the Jamestown area. The English thus clearly demonstrated their intention to take the Americans' lands using every means possible. Unlike the Spanish, the English had no need of American labour, but they foresaw the possibility of the tribes becoming allies in eventual wars against other European powers for the control of the American territories.

The first contacts between the Pilgrims and the native Americans were not dramatic. When the Pilgrims settled in Plymouth, they found the area "a splendid place, suitable for the cultivation of every type of crop". However, they would have died of hunger without the help of Massasoit, chief of the Wampanoag. His authority also prevented the outbreak of war as the colony rapidly expanded towards the interior.

The first problems the Pilgrims had arose with the Pequot, a powerful tribe that lived in the Massachusetts area. The Pilgrims attacked one of their villages and massacred all the inhabitants. All the English colonies along the Atlantic coast, between present-day New York City and Boston, were dragged into the war against the Pequot. Several rival tribes also took part in the war.

Another more important war broke out in 1675 between the colonies and the Wampanoag chief, Metacom, who had also taken an English name. Since he was a chief, he was known as King Philip. The war was caused by English attempts to subjugate the Wampanoag. Metacom was the first native American chief to attempt to unite the tribes against the colonists. He failed, but his example was not forgotten. Later, others tried, with varying degrees of success. Overall, this war – King Philip's War – between the English and the Americans was the bloodiest in the history of the New England colonies. Metacom and his followers destroyed sixteen towns in Massachusetts and four in Rhode Island, and his warriors killed about six hundred colonists. In the end, though, the English prevailed. Metacom was killed, and his wife and son were sold into slavery.

Metacom's idea to unite the tribes was not completely original. In the late 1500s the League of the Iroquois had been formed. Its power was never surpassed by any other American organization. At the end of the seventeenth century, this league dominated the region stretching from the Ottawa River in the north to the Cumberland River in the south, and between Maine in the east and Lake Michigan in the west. The league was so strong that both the English and French sought its support during the Seven Years' War, called in America the French and Indian War.

Opposite page: One of Metacom's greatest victories was the attack and destruction of the village of Sudbury, Massachusetts. The inhabitants were all killed. Captain Samuel Wadsworth pursued the native Americans but was killed in an ambush.

Centre: Yoked Africans are whipped into slavery. The Portuguese voyages of exploration in Africa marked the beginning of the slave trade. The white merchants usually bought slaves from the rulers of the coastal states. The slaves were captured in organized raids into the interior villages.

Top: A brass plate from West Africa showing a Portuguese soldier (Benin, sixteenth century). Until the mid-sixteenth century, the slave trade remained in the hands of the Portuguese. They had commercial bases scattered along the coastal strip of West Africa.

Below: A golden Ashanti mask dating from the fifteenth century (*London, Hartford House*). Ashanti was an African kingdom that originated in the eleventh century. The slave ships set sail from its coast.

THE SLAVE TRADE

African Slaves

The Portuguese voyages of exploration and discovery in Africa also marked the beginning of the slave trade with the western hemisphere. Until the mid-sixteenth century, this traffic remained in the hands of the Portuguese who had bases all along the west coast of Africa. The contractors who supplied the slave ships operated from there. As a general rule, the white slave merchants did not procure the slaves directly but bought them from the rulers of the states along the coast. These rulers organized raids on the villages in the interior or even sold their own subjects to the Europeans in return for firearms.

The unfortunate captives were forced aboard ships to face a terrible voyage. Below decks, they were crammed into holds no more than a metre in height. The slaves were chained together and had very little space in which to move around. The ships were designed to carry the largest possible cargo. The slaves were crammed in this way, not only to ensure the highest profit per voyage, but also to give them the least physical opportunity to revolt. In such conditions, between 20 and 30 per cent of the human cargo died from privation, illness and severe beating. There were also many cases of both individual and mass suicides.

The Spanish government did not want to be directly involved in the slave trade. However, the Spanish granted contracts for the importation of slaves, charging a tax for every slave who entered their American dominions. The slave trade from Africa to America grew as the cultivation of sugarcane increased. African slaves also replaced South American Indian labourers, whose numbers had been drastically reduced by ill treatment, hard work in the mines and the ravages of disease.

With the increase in demand – a direct consequence of the extermination of native Americans – the slave trade flourished. A "triangular trade" was established. European manufactured goods were sent to Africa where

A plan showing how slaves were loaded on a slave ship. The purpose was to cram in the greatest number of people.

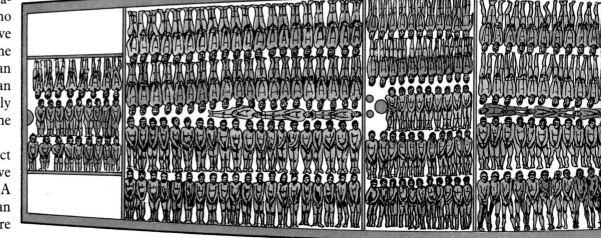

An African mask worn for ritual dances. The slaves took with them to America their tribal customs and beliefs which became part of a new New World culture.

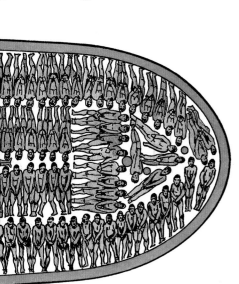

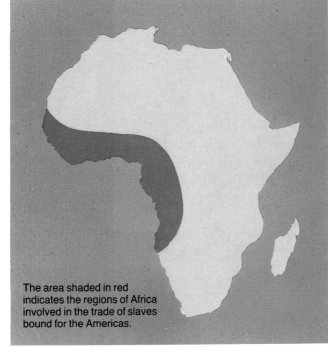

The area shaded in red indicates the regions of Africa involved in the trade of slaves bound for the Americas.

they were exchanged for slaves, who were then sold in the Americas. The final stage was the acquisition of American raw materials from the colonies for importation to Europe. Gradually, the Portuguese slave ships were joined by Dutch, French, Danish and Swedish vessels.

The Employment of Slaves in Latin America

The way the slaves were distributed throughout different parts of America depended on the type of economy in each region. African labour was used on the sugar, cotton and tobacco plantations. The slaves also worked in the mines. Many others worked as domestic servants and in various crafts. The slave-owners seldom cared about the health of their slaves. In mines situated in the high mountains, many slaves from the tropical regions of Africa fell victim to disease. Africans found the climates of the Caribbean islands and the coastal plains of South America more hospitable. In the West Indies, African slaves replaced the indigenous population, almost all of whom had been killed off. In the high Andes, by contrast, few African slaves survived.

It is difficult to calculate exactly how many Africans arrived in America during the years of the slave trade. It may have been as many as fifteen million. Some European voices were raised in protest against slavery, but even reformers such as the Spanish priest Bartolomé de Las Casas were, at first, in favour of slavery as a way of alleviating the plight of the native Americans.

Slaves in North America

Slavery began in North America in the early 1600s, and the traffic in slaves increased very rapidly after 1700. Originally, slaves were brought in from the West Indies, but by the 1670s slaves were being imported directly from Africa.

Living conditions for slaves on many plantations in the English colonies were extremely degrading. Many slaves lived in communal barrack-like shacks, where it was impossible to live a normal family life. In time, the increase of the black population led to the development of more stable plantation communities. Some second- and third-generation African Americans did other forms of work, on farms or in towns. Their culture was a mixture of traditional African and European-colonial elements. From these roots, it became part of the national culture of the American people.

Below: The Spanish captain, Juan Pardo, meeting an American Indian chief in Florida. The Spanish occupation of Florida began during the second half of the sixteenth century.

Map: The map shows the location of the Franciscan missions along the coast of California. The missionary orders played an important role in the exploration of the central and northern regions, often preceding the arrival of the Spanish army. In some regions the missions were the only European presence. The sketch shows the basic design of a mission.

Left: A wooden tabernacle from a California convent church. The native American population helped to build and decorate the mission churches and buildings. Local craft workers combined their traditional techniques and decorations with elements from the Christian religion.

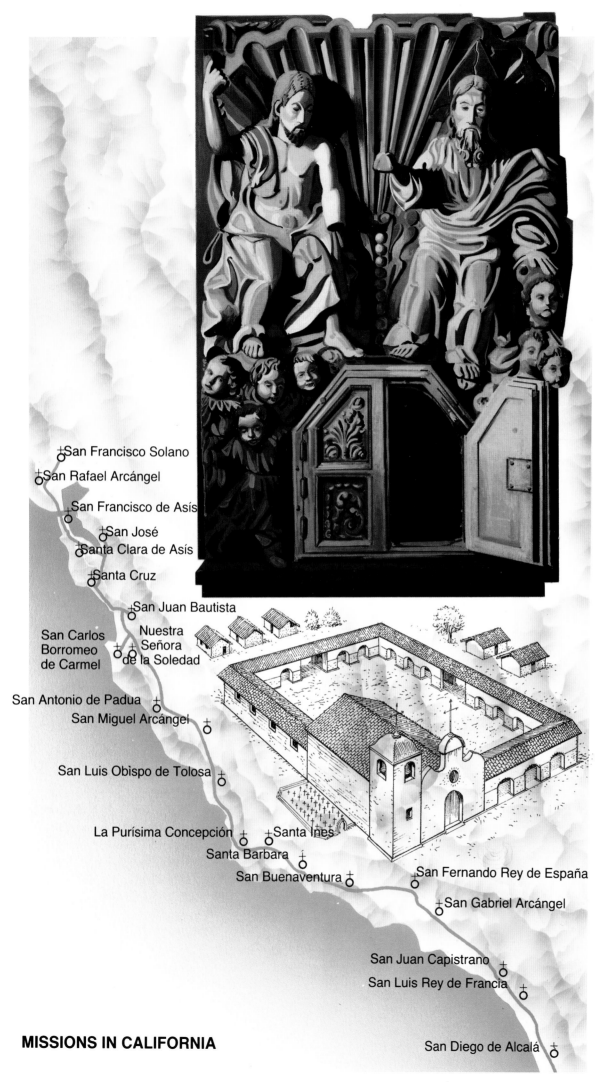

San Francisco Solano

San Rafael Arcángel

San Francisco de Asís

San José
Santa Clara de Asís

Santa Cruz

San Juan Bautista

San Carlos Borromeo de Carmel

Nuestra Señora de la Soledad

San Antonio de Padua

San Miguel Arcángel

San Luis Obispo de Tolosa

La Purísima Concepción

Santa Inés

Santa Barbara

San Buenaventura

San Fernando Rey de España

San Gabriel Arcángel

San Juan Capistrano

San Luis Rey de Francia

San Diego de Alcalá

MISSIONS IN CALIFORNIA

THE SPANISH IN NORTH AMERICA

The rise of strong nations in northern Europe marked the beginning of the end of Spain's "golden age". However, the Spanish managed to expand and defend their American dominions. In the seventeenth century, the northern European powers had only a marginal interest in the Americas. Wars with one another, as well as internal conflicts, distracted them from paying more attention to the Americas and from taking advantage of the vulnerable Spanish position there.

Florida was explored by the Spanish during the second half of the sixteenth century. Several conquistadors and missionaries explored the interior of this southeastern region of North America without establishing any kind of permanent settlement. It was, however, of strategic importance, because Spanish fleets, bound for Spain, sailed near Florida's western coasts.

When the French moved into the area in 1564 and founded Fort Caroline at the mouth of the St. Johns River, Spanish occupation of Florida became imperative. The following year, the Spanish established a fort which they named St. Augustine. Today St. Augustine is the oldest permanent European settlement in North America.

Missionaries played an important role in the consolidation of the Spanish dominions. The Franciscans sent out missionary-explorers from Florida. The missionaries ranged as far north as South Carolina and west to the southern end of the Appalachian Mountains.

Northern Mexico

The search for new silver mines was the direct cause of Spanish expansion into northern Mexico. These mines were situated in the semi-arid prairies along the eastern flank of the Sierra Madre. The region was populated by nomadic Indians. As in Florida, the Franciscans spearheaded the Spanish advance, winning the friendship of the Indians. During the sixteenth century, this area was opened to colonization, and mines were developed at Durango, Charcas, San Luis Potosí and Parral. Farms were started in the more accessible valleys where water was plentiful. These farms grew corn and grain crops to feed the miners. Cattle ranches began to prosper in the drier areas. Frequently, the mine owners also owned the farms and ranches. Their descendants managed to keep and increase their lands, transforming them into huge estates called *haciendas*. The hacienda housed the owner's family, together with priests, overseers, craft workers, *vaqueros* (cowboys) and domestic servants. Spanish expansion in northern Mexico was strongly stimulated by the ambition to create vast estates.

Towards the middle of the seventeenth century, the Spanish crown granted substantial financial help for the colonization of the state of Nuevo Leon in northern Mexico. Missions and military garrisons were built also in eastern Texas, which the Spanish were later forced to abandon due to local American resistance.

Baja (Lower) California

The missionary orders played a key role in the Spanish expansion into both northwestern Mexico and Baja California. The Franciscans, followed by colonists, reached the upper Rio Grande. The Jesuits followed the Sonora River as far north as Arizona.

The Jesuits also established missions in Baja California, where the coastal waters had been famed for pearls since the time of Cortés. The Spanish government encouraged colonization, but settlers were discouraged by the near-desert country.

New Mexico was also colonized by the Spanish, but Indian revolts regularly drove away colonists and the missionaries. The repression of the American resistance in New Mexico was a long struggle.

Emigrants to the English colonies of North America came from a variety of backgrounds, as this map shows.

- English
- Dutch
- French
- German
- Irish
- Scottish
- African

This porcelain dish was made in New England in the seventeenth century by a German emigrant.

ANGLO-AMERICAN SOCIETY IN THE EIGHTEENTH CENTURY

An iron oil lamp. (*Pennsylvania, seventeenth century*)

A New England farm. Life on colonial farms was very hard for all, owners and servants alike. Everyone worked to live.

By the beginning of the eighteenth century, colonists from England had established themselves on the North American continent. The English colonies formed an almost continuous line along the Atlantic coast from New Hampshire to Georgia. Some colonists had explored inland, usually by following rivers. The population at this time was around 250,000. The inhabitants were of European or African birth, or descent, and for the most part, English-speaking. However, the population of the colonies was not evenly distributed. It was concentrated along the Atlantic coast and in the river valleys. Many areas remained uninhabited and uncultivated by Europeans. Even in the older colonies of Massachusetts and Virginia, the colonists for the most part continued to live like frontier pioneers. By the 1700s many colonists had been born on American soil. The colony was their homeland, even though they knew their grandfathers had come from a more powerful European nation much farther away. If they did not yet think of themselves as Americans, they had a way of life that was increasingly different from the European model.

The English Americans

Some American colonists were wealthy, with aristocratic connections, but most came from humbler backgrounds. They were more often farmhands, unskilled workers and craftspeople. Except in New England, many of the white immigrants had arrived as indentured servants. They had agreed to work for four or more years for a person in return for their ocean passage to the colonies. When they were free of these obligations, they often bought or were entitled to receive land of their own.

Free people in the colonies were much more mobile than they had been in Europe. There were few legal limits to control their movements, and everyone was free to go almost anywhere they wished. The population increased rapidly, while in Europe at this time, national populations grew little, if at all.

The Economy in New England

At first, the New Englanders did not wish to become involved in overseas trade. The Puritans had no desire to keep links with a world they had left behind. They hoped the new communities would soon become economically self-sufficient. However, the attempts to create a self-sufficient economy failed. Around 1650 the Puritans turned to an economic system which relied on overseas trade, and this remained until the American Revolution. The production of flour, fish and timber for building developed rapidly in New England. The commercial prospects this offered soon became clear. These products would not be sold to England (which produced its own) but instead went to France and the Spanish American colonies. New England fish, for example, was sold in Spanish America and in the West Indies. Timber and horses (the colonists' chief power source for transport) were exchanged for sugar-based products which found a ready market both in the colonies and back in England.

Other regions became involved in this circle of trade. Virginia produced tobacco; New England became an important source of fish; New York and Pennsylvania produced a variety of agricultural products. The commercial system developed in New England, with certain variations, was adopted by all the northern colonies.

Several circumstances made this trade vigorous but difficult to forecast. Local production of the goods to be sold was irregular. Bad harvests were frequent. Furthermore, it was difficult to know exactly how much could be sold in the West Indies.

In this easy-going colonial world anyone could set up a business, as there were no legal barriers to prevent their doing so. The government encouraged the growth of trade.

The Economy of the Southern Colonies

The early economy of the southern colonies was based on tobacco. Low prices and unforeseeable variations in both the production of tobacco and the market for it made it a rather risky business. The tobacco trade was in the hands of merchants from London who penalized the planters if crops failed. Tobacco production depended on a large work force, and slavery seemed the obvious solution to this need for field hands.

In the Anglo-American world it was often difficult to preserve social differences. In the farm communities, in both northern and southern colonies, there were few distinctions of wealth or class. Everyone was a pioneer.

ART IN LATIN AMERICA

The church of St. Francis at Acatepec in Mexico. The Mexican baroque style is typified by the eye-catching decoration of surfaces, a combination of Spanish and native American artistic experiences. The small picture (*below right*) is a detail of the decoration in a Spanish church in Ecuador (St. Francis, Quito), showing the influence of European and native American styles.

Latin American Baroque

The term baroque indicates an artistic style popular in Europe, and subsequently, in America during the seventeenth century. The origin of the term is not clear. It would appear to derive from the Portuguese word *barroco* – a type of irregularly shaped pearl, having many facets. When applied to painting, sculpture and architecture, the term baroque indicated a style that paid little attention to proportion, but was rich in ornamentation.

The baroque style spread rapidly in Europe in the seventeenth century, and was particularly popular in Italy and Spain. Baroque buildings were much more flamboyant than the buildings of earlier times. Surfaces were covered with elaborate designs and carvings. In Spain and Portugal, the baroque style combined with the rather flat-sided building style current at the time. This resulted in buildings with extravagantly decorated facades. These styles were copied in Spanish- and Portuguese-ruled America.

Latin American Colonial Art

American art grew out of European and native roots. The European migrants to the New World brought with them the cultural heritage of Romanesque, Gothic and Renaissance art. Regional American styles developed throughout the seventeenth century as new ideas from Europe combined with elements of native American and other local artistic styles.

The colonial art of Latin America was not, therefore, the mere transfer of European styles to the New World. The natural artistic gifts of the native Americans, their sense of form and colour, and the colonists' fascination with a landscape so different from Europe tended to modify the artistic styles imported from the Old World.

The European version of baroque architecture is complex. It depends on the principles of optical illusion. Buildings in Spanish America have a relatively simple structure but are more elaborately decorated.

The originality of the Latin American baroque style is often to be found in its ornamental details. For example, the habit of decorating shields with feathers was maintained. The Americans' skill in working with precious metals led to the creation of extravagant jewellery. The interiors of buildings together with decorative objects were often enriched with magnificent inlay work. In fact, the Latin American baroque style found its most original expression in the decoration of wood.

The Latin American baroque style was used above all in religious art. Religion and colonization were closely linked in Latin America. The missionary orders reached into many regions, and the Franciscans, Dominicans, Augustinians and Jesuits played an important part in the history of colonization.

Mexican Baroque

Mexican baroque can be recognized by the eye-catching decoration of surfaces, the result of the artistic tradition, developed before Columbus arrived in America. The local influences combined with the Spanish flat-sided building style. A typical example of this fusion of styles is the cathedral completed in 1661 in Mexico City.

Mexican baroque was the first original colonial Mexican style of art. Previously, Spanish-Mexican art had mostly copied art forms imported from Europe.

Below: A reconstruction of a typical Central American city, built in the baroque style. Spanish rules for colonial cities prescribed a regular chessboard-like plan, but these rules were not always followed.

BAROQUE ART IN SPANISH AND PORTUGUESE AMERICA

The Sculptors of Quito

In Spanish South America, the province of Quito occupied the territory of present-day Ecuador. Less than fifty years before the Spanish conquest, the city of Quito was the second capital of the Inca Empire. The other was Cuzco. The Franciscans were the first to settle in the province. In 1530 the Convent of St. Francis was founded. A college destined to educate the sons of the more important local Americans was annexed to the convent. The curriculum included instruction in and practice of several art forms, and of sculpture in particular.

The most famous artist in Quito was the sculptor Bernardo Legarda, who had a workshop beside the Franciscan monastery. Legarda created the statue that decorates the high altar in the monastery church. Many of his works were dedicated to the Virgin Mary. At this time in Catholic countries, visions of saints were a part of religious life, and many artists prepared themselves for their work with prayer and fasting. Incidents from the life of the Virgin Mary were very popular subjects among artists. The artists of Quito were particularly fond of the themes surrounding the story of the Virgin's Assumption into Heaven.

Legarda produced his work in the first half of the eighteenth century. The most important sculptor from Quito during the second half of the century was Caspicara. His real name was Manuel Chili, and his parents were native Americans. Even though many aspects of his work are similar to the work of Legarda, there is no clear evidence that Caspicara was actually a student of the earlier sculptor. However, the continuity of style between the two artists demonstrates the mastery of the sculpting skills taught in Quito during the period 1700–1730.

Caspicara lived at a time when porcelain and ivory ornaments were highly appreciated decorations in colonial houses. Many of his works are busts or groups of figures. For this reason, he is considered more of an innovator than Legarda, who mostly produced single figures.

Caspicara's most important work is the Assumption, which decorates the altar dedicated to St. Anthony in the Church of St. Francis, in Quito. In this work Caspicara showed he was capable of giving a unifying theme to a group of sculptured figures, while producing richly detailed single figures at the same time. Caspicara's work in general gives the impression of movement.

Baroque Art in Brazil

For a long time Brazil remained a colony of little importance, valued only for its high quality timber. The Portuguese found this land disappointing compared with the rest of Latin America, and there was very little active settlement. This explains why early Brazilian colonial architecture was much plainer than the architecture of colonial Spanish America, until the baroque era. The baroque period coincided with the discovery of precious metals in Brazil. The products of the mines – silver and gold – were used to decorate churches and other buildings.

The Brazilian city of Ouro Prêto (Black Gold) has many excellent examples of the use of gold and silver in works of art. The city was named after the gold found in the black rocks of the surrounding hills. Its thirteen churches, numerous public buildings, decorated fountains and pleasant avenues, linking the hills to the city, make it an open-air museum of Portuguese colonial style. Many houses are adorned with figures and have window frames resembling those found in eighteenth-century churches. When they were built, the balconies had railings and wooden shutters that formed geometric patterns. Glazed tiles were imported from Portugal and the Netherlands. They were used because of the shiny appearance they gave to roofs. One of the city prisons is so well decorated that the iron bars at the windows are hardly noticeable.

The splendour of these buildings is witness to the mastery of the local craftsmen. Their skill is especially evident in the Church of St Francis of Assisi, in Ouro Prêto. A plan of this church is shown right.

Craftsmen from Quito produced works like this richly decorated pulpit in the Church of St. Francis, Quito, Ecuador.

Top left: A column from the facade of a Jesuit church in Quito. *Top right:* An ornamental altar column from the Church of St. Francis in Quito.

A sixteenth-century cross, set with emeralds. (*Central Bank Museum, Ecuador*)

Quito, Ecuador.
The cloister of the Church of St. Francis.

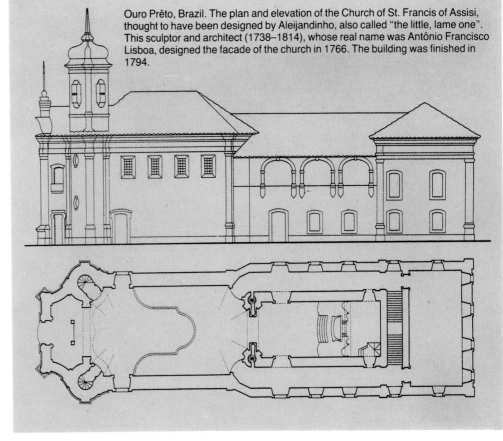

Ouro Prêto, Brazil. The plan and elevation of the Church of St. Francis of Assisi, thought to have been designed by Aleijandinho, also called "the little, lame one". This sculptor and architect (1738–1814), whose real name was Antônio Francisco Lisboa, designed the facade of the church in 1766. The building was finished in 1794.

SPANISH AMERICA'S ECONOMY

Farming

Although mining for gold, silver and other metals yielded much wealth, Latin America's chief resource for colonists was its farmland. Much of the region was more suitable for raising livestock than for crop-growing.

The Spanish Americans acquired properties called haciendas, which ranged in size from small farms to vast estates. The most important haciendas were situated in northern Mexico, in the valleys of central Chile and on the slopes of the Andes.

In the more densely populated areas and near the larger towns, the smallest haciendas grew cereal crops and reared a few animals to be sold in the local markets. In the tropical and subtropical regions, the haciendas tended to specialize in cultivating sugar, cacao and indigo.

By the beginning of the seventeenth century, Spanish America had become self-sufficient in the production of wheat and other cereals. The creation of more pastureland meant more cattle, more meat. Vines and olives flourished in the river valleys of Peru and central Chile. These regions produced wines and olive oil of reasonable quality, yet much cheaper than those from European growers. They sold so well in Spain that the Spanish king was pressured by Spanish wine and olive oil producers into curbing any further expansion of the cultivation of wine and olive oil in the Spanish American territories. Their sale into Spain was banned.

Besides the principal foodstuffs, the most important farm products were hides, sugar, cacao, tobacco and cotton. Spanish America was also rich in forest products, such as timber, dyes from bark, flavourings such as vanilla, many types of spices and medicinal plants. Such products formed a large part of the total colonial exports to Europe.

Capital and Industry

The Spanish Americans certainly appreciated the value of money, but among the landowners, old-fashioned attitudes prevailed. The wealthy spent a large proportion of their resources on donations to the church, dowries for their daughters and a luxurious life-style. It was not their custom to trust their money to banks or to buy shares in businesses.

In spite of this attitude, some small businesses developed. Food processing, pottery and the leather goods trade grew to meet local needs. The textile industry underwent the greatest development. There were basically three main reasons for this: the expansion of the internal Spanish American market, the weakness of the textile industry in Spain, and the high cost of textile products imported from Europe.

At the beginning of the seventeenth century, hundreds of workshops throughout the West Indies manufactured clothes and other textile

articles. Ecuador was the main centre of production in South America; it had large numbers of sheep and a large workforce. The textile factories produced woollen cloth, cotton, silk, linen and hemp. The majority were small workshops, privately owned, but in Mexico and Ecuador some were run by native American communities.

The Spanish colonies were self-sufficient in the production of the cheaper textiles, but a variety of circumstances prevented the American textile industry from expanding more fully. The Spanish government issued a series of laws regulating textile production and conditions for the employment of labour. The labour laws were intended to protect the native Americans from exploitation. However, the real reason behind the legislation was the government's desire to reduce competition from the colonial industry in favour of the domestic market. The Spanish Americans invented many ways to avoid the restrictions, but Spain's action certainly slowed down the expansion of industry in the colonies.

Taxation

Interference from Spain had a damaging influence on the development of the economy in Spanish America. Beginning in the reign of Philip II, the government started to tax the Spanish American territories. Driven by the rising costs of wars in Europe, Spain introduced a series of taxes. There was a general sales tax, a tax on stamped paper, on mercury, salt, pepper and on all forms of trade.

Smuggling

Spanish producers were not able to satisfy all the needs of the American market. Furthermore, the goods shipped from Spain were too expensive, while Spain did not buy colonial products at a price high enough to satisfy local producers. This set of circumstances forced many Spanish American traders to start smuggling. Meanwhile, the Dutch and English set up a freewheeling international trading community in the Caribbean area. English, Dutch, French and Spanish merchants traded with one another freely, ignoring government restrictions. Direct trade, bypassing Spain, began to develop between the Spanish American colonies and the northern European nations.

Left: Work in a Cuban sugar refinery. The growing and processing of sugarcane continued to be one of the chief resources of the West Indian economy.

Right: A cattle ranch. Native Americans were employed as cowboys, as the size of beef cattle herds grew steadily. Meat became a major product within Spanish America.

SPANISH AMERICAN SOCIETY

Society in Spanish America was, the early colonists believed, based on class. The class structure was upheld by the law and its divisions (nobles, church, masses) were originally those of the European homeland. However, the American reality was soon somewhat different from what the Europeans had imagined. The Spanish government opposed the creation of a powerful class of nobles in Spanish America. Furthermore, there was no category in the traditional class system that might include non-Europeans, that is to say, the majority of the American population.

For these reasons, while the social order in Spanish America did have a class structure, the distinctions were based on race. The Spanish considered themselves physically different from native Americans, from Africans and from those of mixed backgrounds. Physical and cultural differences justified, in their eyes, severe forms of discrimination between the groups.

Independent of their class or origin, the Spanish considered themselves the direct descendants of the conquistadors. They believed in their own racial and cultural superiority. Legally, they enjoyed several privileges. The *encomenderos*, who were more or less the heirs of the conquerors and the first colonists, formed the most aristocratic group in Spanish colonial society. A new aristocracy had emerged among the owners of the haciendas. Owning land was no automatic guarantee of prestige and honour, but it was the necessary condition to begin climbing the social ladder. The great landowners had a stable workforce, lived for part of the year in town mansions, and ran local government.

The old and new aristocratic groups occasionally came together through marriage. In this way the encomenderos acquired haciendas, while the hacienda-owners became related to families longer established than their own. As the haciendas became larger and more numerous, owning land became the most common way to be accepted as part of the nobility.

The Middle and Lower Classes

Merchants held the highest position in the social scale among the Spanish who did not belong to landed or noble families. The rich importers and silver merchants of Mexico City and Lima formed associations that dealt directly with the representatives of the Spanish king in America. These mercantile associations financed the construction of hospitals, orphanages and roads.

As a Spanish-speaking middle class emerged, lawyers became an important group of profes-sional people. Legal business boomed.

Below the merchants and lawyers came craftsmen, shopkeepers, small farmers and domestic servants. The lowest class was made up of poor labourers and vagrants.

The Clergy and the Royal Bureaucracy

From the seventeenth century the power of the Roman Catholic church in Latin America increased enormously. The foundation of new cities and the development of those already in existence required the creation of new parishes. The church also owned a great deal of land. The church in South America became the most powerful religious organization.

The representatives in Spanish America of the king of Spain enjoyed similar high-ranking status. These officials were often ennobled on their return to Spain.

A Spanish American wedding. Marriage was often a means of uniting the old aristocracy of the *encomenderos* with the new aristocracy, formed by the hacienda-owners.

A beautifully decorated, lacquered plate. (Seventeenth century, Ecuador.)

NATIVE AMERICANS AND OTHER PEOPLES

The Native Americans

On the whole, the Spanish considered native Americans not only uncivilized and ignorant, but also lazy, unreliable and incapable of becoming true Christians. The Spanish literally looked down on most of the so-called Indians, who were smaller than the average European. Their hair was straight, and their skin was darker than that of the Spanish.

Under colonial rule, the Indians had to pay taxes to their masters, and their freedom of movement was limited by law. However, in response to the rapid decline of the native population, the Spanish government expressed concern for the welfare of the remaining Americans and gave them special status as wards of the monarchy. The Spanish king appointed high ranking civil and church officials as "protectors" of the Indians. Special courts were set up to deal with trials involving disputes between Indians and Spanish or proceedings between Indians.

The Indian population, shattered by the conquest, clung to a weakening social structure. The highest class was composed of the descendants of the ancient aristocracy in pre-Columbian times. The Spanish government recognized these nobles, granting them a few privileges and immunity from some restrictions. However, this class gradually lost its importance, the aristocrats became poorer, and it was increasingly difficult to distinguish them from the rest of the native American population.

The bulk of the native Americans fell into two groups. The largest was made up of those obliged by law to live in fixed communities and to pay taxes. The second group consisted of people who fled their villages and settled on the outskirts of towns, cities or on the haciendas as farm labourers.

Mestizos, Free Blacks and Slaves

By the end of the seventeenth century there had been two centuries of mingling between races in the Americas. There were three recognized mixed-race groups: mestizos, children of Europeans and Indians; mulattoes, children of European and African parents; and zambos, children of Indian and African parents. The Spanish regarded all mixed-race people as a single class – seen as idle vagrants, landless, and a threat to religion and public order. The more their numbers grew, the more Europeans' fear increased. Efforts by mestizos, mulattoes and zambos to settle, find jobs, and establish themselves in society were regarded with suspicion by the whites.

These different groups were treated by the Spanish government in a similar way to the American Indians. They were obliged to pay taxes, and their freedom of movement was very limited. They also were not allowed to carry weapons or go to a university.

Although slavery of the Indians continued in secret until the 1700s, the majority of slaves were blacks and mulattoes. Even though all slaves were considered the same by law, among the slaves themselves there was a kind of class system. Those who lived as servants in the houses of the rich Spanish, together with artisans, were higher-ranking socially than slaves who worked in the mines.

How Changes Were Made

Social and class differences were well fixed in both Spanish law and the Spanish mentality, but they were not unchangeable. Slaves could achieve freedom in various ways. They could buy their freedom by paying a certain sum of money or be declared free if their master was proved guilty under the law of mistreating them.

Social class was determined not only by the colour of a person's skin, but also by their way of life. Some mestizo families managed to mix with members of the Spanish lower classes. The practical needs of government also contributed to social levelling. In order to increase the army, for example, the rules forbidding the recruitment of persons of mixed background or of blacks were waived. As a general rule, the whiter the skin, the easier it was for a person to move upwards in society. However, access to the privileged peaks of the Spanish American world remained largely impossible for non-whites.

Even after the native Americans' conversion to Roman Catholicism, ancient rituals survived throughout Latin America.

Far left: A native American medicine man leading a pagan ceremony. Traditional and European beliefs and customs became interwoven. Many Indians became Christians but their forms of worship had a distinctly traditional flavour.

Right: The Flying Dancers of the Totonacs of Mexico still enthrall tourists today. The man on top of the pole is the captain of a team and represents the sun. At his signal, four men seated at his feet launch themselves backwards into the air. They are held by strong ropes. They represent the four basic elements: earth, air, water and fire. Since the conversion of the tribe to Roman Catholicism, this pre-Christian festival is celebrated on the anniversary of the birth of St. Francis of Assisi.

THE CREOLES

The Spanish and the Creoles

Spanish settlers in America who had been born in Europe called the American-born Spanish Creoles. They looked down on the Creoles, believing that being born in the Americas automatically made a person inferior. The Creoles, not surprisingly, were offended by this arrogant, patronizing attitude, typical of most of the new Spanish arrivals in the colonies. Moreover, they resented the ease with which

these Spaniards often managed to acquire important positions and other advantages, which by law should have been open to them.

The Creoles

The first Spanish who arrived in America were self-confident and ambitious. The conquerors dreamed of returning to Spain with glory, fame and riches, and of becoming landowners and aristocrats. But the spoils of

the conquest fell below expectations for many, and they remained in America, to seek their fortunes.

The descendants of the conquerors were true Latin Americans, not Europeans. They were called Creoles, and in a sense they bridged the gulf between Old and New Worlds. The Creoles' houses were filled with sounds foreign to Spanish ears. Their Castilian Spanish was mixed with native American and African words

A colonial villa in Spanish America. The white master is giving orders to black slaves. A black nurse, carrying the master's son, chats with a mestizo domestic servant.

Spain. The Creoles aimed at creating a Creole spirit, a pride in being a Spanish American, and a freedom from an inferiority complex regarding Spain.

The Creole identity was especially evident in religion. The Creoles thought themselves the most devout of all Catholics. A great deal of their time was spent at mass and other services. They made donations to their parishes or local convents and gave gifts to charitable institutions. During the seventeenth century, a series of apparently miraculous recoveries from illness and reports of religious visions led the Creoles to believe that God had decided to reward them for their devotion to the faith. In 1671 the first American saint was canonized. There were Creole bishops and Creole church officials.

Regional Differences

The native American culture survived to a greater extent in the high plateaus, where people were left alone to preserve the old ways. Creole society developed independent of Europe in these remote regions too. On the plains and in the areas near the ports, the Creoles tended to keep stronger ties with Europe, due to their dependence on sea trade.

The most elaborate societies were found in the high river basins and valleys of the great mountain ranges. These regions were inhabited by large numbers of Indians and mestizos. These regions, however, were dominated by a white minority of powerful aristocratic families who held the land.

On the plains the population was mixed. The plains were the poorest areas, where social differences arising from wealth were less evident.

and accents. As babies they were cared for by native American wet nurses, and as children they ate food with exotic local ingredients. Native herbalists calmed Creole fevers with ointments and herbal teas, and native artists decorated Creole churches with pictures of the animals and plants of the Americas. However, the Creoles felt a certain nostalgia for Spain, mixed with a sense of inferiority because they could not consider it their real native land.

They also felt some antipathy towards new arrivals from Europe.

The Creoles began to develop their own culture. Creole writers expressed their pride in being born in the Americas and celebrated their way of life. They praised the beauty of their cities, the splendour of their buildings and churches, and the success of their commerce. The Creole writers affirmed that American culture had no reason to envy the culture of

BRAZIL

Brazil and Portugal

The colonial government in Brazil was military, dominated by the governors and their subordinates. During the eighteenth century, when exploitation of the rich Brazilian gold mines began, the Portuguese government attempted to control the political and economic life of the colony more closely. Overall, though, the government in Brazil was smaller and less developed than in Spanish America.

Brazilian Colonial Society: The Ruling Classes

The coastal regions where sugarcane was cultivated, from Pernambuco to Rio de Janeiro, were the most highly developed areas of the colony. The Portuguese made up the dominant class. Within these regions, the owners of the plantations controlled affairs and were appointed to the government positions. The officials sent by the government in Portugal enjoyed privileges and titles that set them above the other social groups, but they did not have the power to dominate the local aristocracy.

Immediately below this class in Portuguese American society came the middle class, made up of the merchants involved in foreign trade. They lived in the ports and were usually of European birth. They were not the richest members of society, and were not the social equals of the plantation owners. However, the most wealthy among them purchased land or married into one of the land-holding families and became part of the landed aristocracy. The plantation owner-merchant, who divided his time between his activities on the plantation and the demands of the market, became an important person.

The most modest European social class in colonial Brazil was made up of shopkeepers, craftsmen, accountants, small farmers and the overseers and machine-minders who worked on the plantations. As in Spanish America, Brazilian society was deeply divided by birth – notably between the Portuguese born in America, or Creoles, and those born in Europe.

The Creoles were Brazilians, becoming less

Large Brazilian plantations were called *fazendas*. The great fazenda owners made up the dominant class in Brazil. They controlled the local government.

and less Portuguese. The Portuguese language they spoke included more and more words of American and African origin. Their African cooks used the plants and meats of the New World to invent a new Brazilian cuisine. African colours, sounds and musical rhythms were present in the religious celebrations of the colony and continue to this day.

Race and Slavery

Both the Creoles and the Portuguese born in Europe considered the Africans and native Americans "inferiors". These prejudices led to the condemnation of marriages between Europeans and Africans or native Americans and to the restriction of movement and freedom of choice regarding work.

The children of native Americans and Portuguese suffered less racial discrimination than the children of Africans and Portuguese. They were free and occupied a place in the social scale above free blacks and mulattoes, who were not allowed to occupy positions in the church or in the civil government. The lowest class was formed by black and mulatto slaves.

People of African origin were more numerous in Brazil than in Spanish America. Slaves often escaped and fled to the interior of Brazil where they formed large communities. Ten large groups of this type existed in the interior. The strongest group called their territory the Republic of Palmares. The inhabitants built stockades with houses inside the walls. They created an artificial lake, well supplied with fish. The refuge that Palmares offered to slaves from the plantations represented such a threat to the owners of the great plantations in Pernambuco that the army was forced to intervene. The settlement resisted and fell only after a siege lasting forty days in 1697.

A different type of society developed in the northern Brazilian hinterland and on the southern plateaus. These vast regions of dry scrub and grassland were populated by Europeans, Africans and native Americans, who intermingled.

The Portuguese reached the Amazon region at the beginning of the seventeenth century and during the following years consolidated their claims to the Amazon River basin. A few scattered settlements appeared. The settlers were merchants, both of Portuguese or mixed background, people seeking to trade in forest products (such as timber and animal skins), and missionaries. The native forest tribes mostly preserved their freedom, though some groups came under European influence.

A street in São Luis do Maranhão, Brazil. Royal officials lived in the city and also landowners who kept houses there, from where they did business, selling their plantation products.

MISSIONARIES IN THE AMERICAS

Latin America was the setting for an intensive missionary campaign by the Roman Catholic church. Two institutions created to assist in the work of converting Americans were called (in Spanish) the *doctrina* and the *congregación*. The doctrina was a school for religious instruction run by monks or nuns. Some young people were accepted as boarders and received a more intensive type of training. They were in turn expected to help teach their own people.

The congregaciónes were native American communities organized by the missionaries. Apart from facilitating their religious conversion, these communities aimed at transforming the Americans' way of life. The missionaries intended to make the Indians adopt European habits. They were supposed to learn to eat at tables, to sleep in beds and to wear clothes.

The missionaries also built hospitals to treat the sick, and to offer shelter to travellers and poor people.

The missionaries encountered numerous difficulties. The regions entrusted to the monks were too vast to be controlled easily. The Indians often refused to abandon their traditional homes and those who were forced to enter the Christian communities often fled. The missionaries regularly quarrelled with landowners because the missionaries saved the Indians in their care from exploitation.

The Jesuits in America

The Society of Jesus was founded in Spain in 1539. It differed from other missionary orders in its lack of racial and social prejudice. In fact, its members came from all levels of society. Rather than retreating from the world, the Jesuits aimed at becoming more involved in it. They were especially involved in the education of the young.

The Jesuits arrived in the Americas later than

In their missions, the Franciscans taught the Indians farming skills, how to tan hides and how to improve their traditional crafts.

the other missionary orders. They built on the experience of the congregaciones. They persuaded the Indians to live in groups of villages called *reducciónes*. The name derived from the Latin expression, *reducere ad ecclesiam et vitam civilem*, which means "to lead towards the church and a civil life". A church was built in the centre of the community, and the priests taught their assistants the basic ideas of the faith. To make their task easier, the Jesuits learned the natives' language. The Indians usually lived in the reducciónes but many were reluctant to convert wholeheartedly to Christianity. They often continued to worship their old gods and kept many of their old customs.

At first the reducciónes were founded near the cities. In Brazil, for example, the first communities were created near Bahia, Pernambuco and Rio de Janeiro. These reducciónes were often attacked by Indians who had not been converted and by Portuguese colonists, who wanted to use the Indians of the reducciónes as slaves. Both the Jesuits and the Portuguese government opposed (in theory) the exploitation of Indians. New reducciónes were constructed in regions far away from the European settlements. They were self-sufficient and out of bounds to whites, except for the Jesuits.

This type of community could be found in a vast area including parts of the present-day countries of Paraguay, Uruguay, Argentina and Brazil. Some of the reducciónes were often attacked by armed gangs who destroyed the communities and took the native Americans prisoner. In Paraguay, the Jesuits obtained the Spanish government's permission to arm the Indians under their protection. In 1641 an army of four thousand Guaraní Indians inflicted a crushing defeat on the plunderers. The Jesuit province of Paraguay then began to enjoy a period of calm and prosperity, and by the end of the eighteenth century, there were thirty flourishing reducciónes in the region.

Below: Bandits raiding a reducción to capture the Indians who worked there. The reducciónes were founded by the Jesuits to keep the Indians from being exploited as slaves.

The plan of a reducción. The community was made up of a church, Indian dwellings, storehouses and cultivated fields. The most important Jesuit reducciónes were situated in Colombia, along the upper Orinoco River, in Peru, along the upper reaches of the Amazon and the Marañón, and along the Paraná River in Paraguay.

New Frontiers in North America

In the second half of the seventeenth century, England made a greater effort to control the life and organization of its American colonies. However, the government failed to create one central office responsible for co-ordinating all the government offices with interests in the colonies. The English government remained an accumulation of different government departments, often in conflict with each other, and, consequently, the nation's control over its colonies remained weak. The emerging empire was run on strictly "trade-first" principles. These were translated into law via the Navigation Acts, which attempted to regulate commerce.

In 1760, when George III became king, the colonists celebrated the event with enthusiasm.

The colonists, as subjects of Great Britain, enjoyed the most liberal political conditions in the western world. They foresaw a free and prosperous future. However, during the years of settlement, several areas of conflict had grown between Great Britain and its colonies. The most obvious areas of conflict were caused by the various wars waged by England against other European nations.

The War of Jenkins' Ear and King George's War

In the eighteenth century, Britain fought three wars against the other European powers, and each war also involved the colonies.

The War of Jenkins' Ear (1739–1742) was

fought against the Spanish over trading rights in the colonies in the Caribbean Sea and Central America. With the peace treaty in 1713, which marked the end of the War of the Spanish Succession, Britain had obtained the right to sell certain goods in the Spanish West Indies. The presence of British vessels also brought an increase in smuggling, which the Spanish tried to restrain by stricter cargo inspections. An Englishman, Captain Robert Jenkins, was caught smuggling and had his ear cut off as punishment. War broke out after this episode. A colonial American regiment, led by English officers, was recruited for an expedition against Cartagena, Colombia. Most of the money to finance the expedition was also collected in the American colonies. Due to the incompetence of

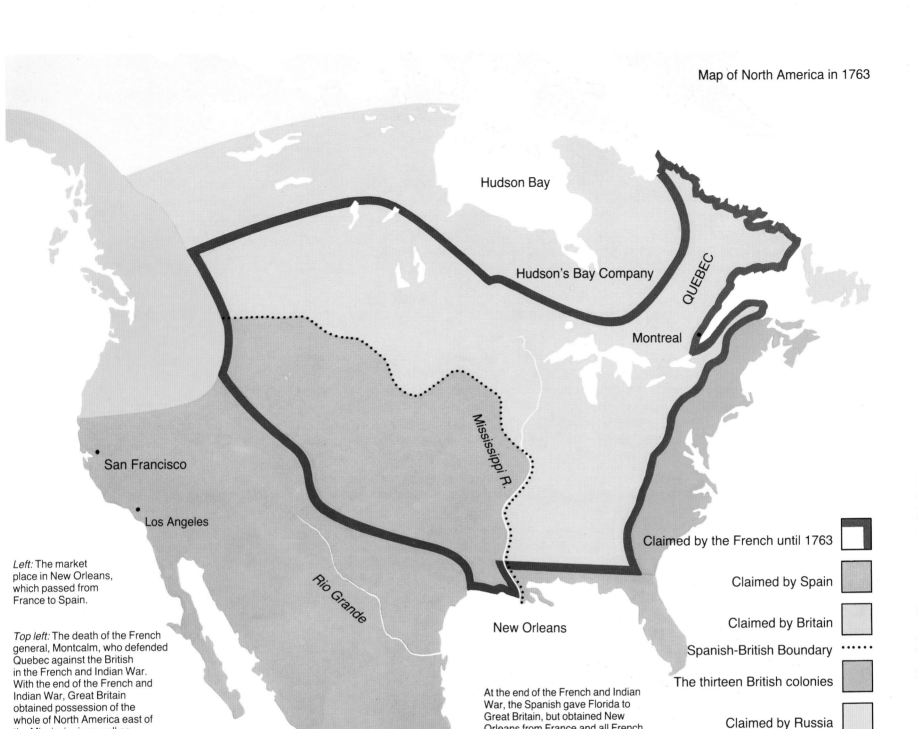

Hudson Bay

Hudson's Bay Company

QUEBEC

Montreal

Mississippi R.

San Francisco

Los Angeles

Rio Grande

New Orleans

Left: The market place in New Orleans, which passed from France to Spain.

Top left: The death of the French general, Montcalm, who defended Quebec against the British in the French and Indian War. With the end of the French and Indian War, Great Britain obtained possession of the whole of North America east of the Mississippi, as well as Canada and Nova Scotia.

At the end of the French and Indian War, the Spanish gave Florida to Great Britain, but obtained New Orleans from France and all French territories west of the Mississippi.

Claimed by the French until 1763

Claimed by Spain

Claimed by Britain

Spanish-British Boundary ······

The thirteen British colonies

Claimed by Russia

the officials, the campaign was a disaster. Only six hundred American soldiers survived.

In 1740 another British war against the Spanish broke out in Europe. Through a complicated series of conflicts and alliances, Great Britain tried to prevent continental Europe from falling under the control of one single power – France. The conflicts between 1740 and 1748 are known in Europe as the War of the Austrian Succession. In America, the conflict was called King George's War (1744–1748).

In America, the war was fought around the French base of Louisbourg on Cape Breton Island. Britain had declared war against France in 1744, and the governor of the Massachusetts colony organized the attack against the fortress of Louisbourg. All the colonies sent equipment and troops, and the Americans captured the French base. It was a great victory for the

colonies. But, when the peace treaty was drawn up in Europe, in exchange for the return of Madras, India, from the French, the British gave Louisbourg back to the French. It seemed as though five hundred Americans had died for nothing to capture the naval base.

The French and Indian War

The French and Indian War between 1756 and 1763 was part of the wider war known as the Seven Years' War. In America, it broke out with a series of clashes between the French and the Virginians over the settlements in the Ohio River valley. The British colonists suffered two years of defeat, but then received fresh troops from Britain and eventually beat the French. To the north, the British captured Quebec and Montreal, to end France's control of Canada.

When the war ended in 1763 Great Britain held undisputed possession of the whole of

North America east of the Mississippi River, excluding New Orleans, but including Canada and Nova Scotia. Spain, which had been France's ally in the war, gave Florida to the British, but obtained New Orleans and territories to the west of the Mississippi.

Great Britain had accumulated an enormous debt to cover the expenses of the war. This debt forced George III to impose new taxes on American colonies. The Americans felt free. Their frontiers were no longer threatened by French or Spanish. The war had given them new confidence, and weakened their respect for Britain. They resented above all the rigid reinforcement of British Navigation Acts which were designed to raise money from the colonies. The merchants and several colonial politicians began to realize that commercial links with Great Britain, as they stood, might be counter to American interests.

THE BRITISH COLONIES ON THE EVE OF INDEPENDENCE

In the British colonies of North America, a century and a half of development had created a vigorous and free-thinking society, though most Americans still saw themselves as "British". In the mid-1700s, the British government began to interfere more forcefully, and imprudently, with the life of the North American colonies. The most obvious cause of tension was the resentment generated by trade laws, which were considered hostile and arbitrary by the Americans. Another important cause of tension was the Americans' feeling that, although in theory they had the same rights as Englishmen, they were not treated as equals – having no voice in parliament.

The Americans

During the period of growth and expansion before George III came to the throne, the Americans gradually became aware of having a separate identity from the British. This difference was not so much embodied in laws or politics, as in the character and culture of the people. The Americans considered themselves honest, innocent, unsophisticated people. Some British politicians shared this view, but judged these characteristics as failings not virtues.

The idea of Americans as simple and innocent people was encouraged by the propaganda used for the recruitment of potential emigrants from Europe to the colonies. For more than a century, leaflets and publications had been circulating in Europe with the aim of attracting emigrants. This form of advertising described the marvels of a simple, benevolent society, where the king's power was reduced and where land could be claimed by anyone willing to farm it. The colonies were seen also as a religious haven where freedom of worship was allowed.

This religious tolerance was symbolized by the success in America of the Puritans and – above all – the Quakers. In the 1680s the members of this religious sect, led by William Penn, had settled the colony of Pennsylvania and founded Philadelphia, "The City of Brotherly Love". Philadelphia prospered. It was open to everyone and became an important cultural centre. Within one generation, Philadelphia became the most dynamic city in the whole of British America, with some ten thousand inhabitants.

During the seventeenth century, the Quakers had been considered religious extremists. They were famous in England for their independent intellectual spirit and for their total refusal to respect governmental authorities. They showed little prejudice and accepted people from all social classes. The atmosphere of the eighteenth century was more tolerant, and the Quakers were no longer regarded as dangerous radicals. They were no longer the fanatical defenders of religious freedom, but they did support religious tolerance and human rights when both were threatened by the arrogance of government.

Pennsylvania, in particular, and British North America as a whole became for Europeans an example of a society free from the hindrance of rigid institutions. It was a society free of the restrictions of Europe, but sophisticated enough to produce individuals of the brilliance of Benjamin Franklin (1706–1790). Franklin was a businessman, writer and scientist: a self-taught genius who won respect in both New and Old Worlds. Franklin represented the essence of America; a young, growing land but able to teach lessons to the Old World.

This picture of a snake chopped in pieces was a piece of propaganda, designed to persuade Americans that the thirteen colonies must unite. It became a famous symbol during the American Revolution.

Right: A New York market place. America's cities were growing. Gradually the Americans began to see themselves as a new nation, with a separate identity from the British, and more freedom. In America anyone could acquire land, live where they wished, and practise the religion of their choice, usually more freely than in Europe.

Below: A Quaker meeting. During the eighteenth century, the Quakers were leading supporters of religious tolerance and human rights.

A caravel.

An Inuit. The northernmost regions of North America remained unexplored by Europeans until the 1800s.

A conquistador.

Walter Raleigh. His efforts led to the foundation of the first English settlement in North America (1585).

Quebec

Montreal

New York • Boston

NORTH AMERICA

Philadelphia

A Quaker.

San Francisco

Los Angeles

New Orleans

A Cuban colonial mansion.

Mexico City

A Mexican church, built by the Jesuits in 1600.

Thirteen colonies

Claimed by Britain

Claimed by Spain

Claimed by Russia

America About 1763

The two maps illustrate the political situation in North and South America, on the eve of the American Revolution (1776) that created the United States of America.

The people and objects illustrated beside the maps symbolize some of the changes that the Europeans brought to the Americas.

Christopher Columbus.

• Quito

• Lima

SOUTH
AMERICA

Pernambuco

Bahia •

Ouro Prêto •

Rio de Janeiro •

• Santiago   • Buenos Aires

A black slave.

Spanish territories

Portuguese territories

British territories

Dutch territories

French territories

Unexplored areas

GLOSSARY

Aleut: a native of the Aleutian Islands and western portion of the Alaskan peninsula

archipelago: a group of many scattered islands

aribal vase: an Inca vase used for transporting liquids

arquebus: early kind of portable gun, supported on a tripod or a forked rest and detonated by a slow-burning match; used before flintlock muskets were invented

artisan: skilled worker in industry or trade

astrolabe: navigational instrument used in the Middle Ages to determine the height of the sun above the horizon

baroque: florid or extravagant style in the arts (especially architecture) in Europe in the seventeenth and eighteenth centuries

bastion: part of a fortification that stands out from the rest; military stronghold near hostile territory

blockhouse: military stronghold with openings through which to shoot

captaincies: a large area in a Portuguese colony given to a person to establish a colony

cinerary urn: a burial urn used in ancient times to preserve the ashes of the dead after cremation

cloister: covered walk on the sides of an open court, especially in the grounds of a monastery, cathedral or college

concession: right given by owner(s) of land, or by a government, to do something on or with the land, for example, to take minerals from the land

conquistador: one of the sixteenth-century Spanish conquerors of Mexico and Peru

Creole: either a person of European descent in Spanish America or, in the West Indies, someone of mixed European and African ancestry

deity: a god or goddess

despot: a ruler with absolute power

edict: order or proclamation issued by an all-powerful authority

facade: (architecture) front or face of a building, towards a street or open place

facet: one of the many sides of a cut stone or jewel

galleon: large sailing ship of the 1500s

Gothic: style of architecture common in Western Europe in the Later Middle Ages, characterized by pointed arches and clusters of columns

hemp: plant from which coarse fibres are obtained for making rope and cloth

hinterland: remote parts of a country away from the coast or a river's banks

indigo: deep blue dye obtained from a plant

Inuit: Native American group, also known as Eskimos, living in northern Canada, Alaska and Greenland; the word means "the people"

manioc: tropical plant with edible, starchy roots

mercantile: relating to trade, commerce and merchants

mestizo: person with one Spanish parent and one native American parent

missionary: someone who goes to convert others to his or her religious faith

mulatto: in the Americas, a person with one white parent and one black parent

native American: another name for the original inhabitants of the Americas, called Indians by the early European explorers

omen: sign of something good or warning of evil fortune

papal bull: official order or announcement from the pope

plantation: large farm given over to one crop, such as tobacco or sugarcane

polygamy: custom of having more than one wife at the same time

pre-Columbian: before Columbus' journey to America

privateer: a privately owned armed ship that, with open or unspoken government approval, attacks the ships, especially merchant ships, of another nation; also, the captain of such a ship

pulpit: raised and enclosed structure in a church, used by a clergyman, especially when preaching

Renaissance: period of revival of art and literature in Europe in the period 1300–1500, when Greek and Roman art was much admired

Romanesque: style of architecture, with round arches and thick walls (in Europe between the classical and Gothic periods)

scurvy: disease common among sailors of the 1500s and 1600s, caused by eating too much salt meat and not enough fresh vegetables and fruit

sextant: navigational instrument used for measuring the altitude of the sun, in order to determine a ship's position

snuff: powdered tobacco, taken into the nose by sniffing

INDEX

A

B

C

F

Falkland Islands, 5
Far East, 8
Far West, 7-8
fazendas, 55
Ferdinand of Aragon, 9, 10, 13
Florida, 38-39, 59
foodstuffs, 41, 46
Fort Caroline, 39
Fort Orange (Albany, NY), 27, 32
France, 11, 25, 41, 59
Franciscans, 38, 39, 43-44, 56
Franklin, Benjamin, 60
French, 8, 10-11, 20, 25, 35, 37, 39, 47, 59
French and Indian War, 35, 59
French Guiana, 25
French Louisiana, 25
Frobisher, Martin, 28

G

galleons, 20-21
galley, 8
Genoa, 8
George III, king of England, 58-60
Goa, 22
Gran Chaco, 5
Granada, 13
Great Bear Lake, 4
Great Lakes, 6, 7, 25
Great Slave Lake, 4
Greenland, 4, 6, 8, 65
Guadeloupe, 25
Guaraní Indians, 5, 57
Guatemala, 13
Guiana (Surinam), 27
Guiana Highlands, 4
Gulf of Guayaquil, 15
Gulf of Mexico, 4

H

haciendas, 39, 46, 48, 50
Harlem River, 33
Hartford, 31, 36
Havana, 18
Hawkins, John, 28
Henry VIII, king of England, 28
Hispaniola, 4, 9-10, 19
Holland, 20-21, 30 *See also* Netherlands
Honduras, 7, 13
Hopewell, 4
Hopi, 34
horses, 13, 15, 41
Huascar, 15
Huayna Capac, Inca, 14-15
Hudson, Henry, 25, 27, 32-33
Hudson Bay, 4, 59
Hudson River, 25, 27
Hudson's Bay Company, 59

I

Iceland, 8
Incas, 6-7, 14-15
indentured servants, 41
India, 8, 22, 26, 59
Indian Ocean, 22
Indonesia, 22, 26
Inuit, 6, 62
Iowa (Indians), 34
Ipiutak, 7
Irish, 40
Iroquois, 35
Isabella of Castile, 9-10, 13

J

Jamaica, 11
James River, 28